T0209984

# HIKING THE MOUNTAIN
# IN FLIP-FLOPS

*Diana Sumner*

**BALBOA**.PRESS

A DIVISION OF HAY HOUSE

Balboa Press books may be ordered through booksellers or by contacting:

Balboa Press
A Division of Hay House
1663 Liberty Drive
Bloomington, IN 47403
www.balboapress.com
1 (877) 407-4847

Because of the dynamic nature of the Internet, any web addresses or
links contained in this book may have changed since publication and
may no longer be valid. The views expressed in this work are solely those
of the author and do not necessarily reflect the views of the publisher,
and the publisher hereby disclaims any responsibility for them.

The author of this book does not dispense medical advice or prescribe the use
of any technique as a form of treatment for physical, emotional, or medical
problems without the advice of a physician, either directly or indirectly. The
intent of the author is only to offer information of a general nature to help
you in your quest for emotional and spiritual well-being. In the event you use
any of the information in this book for yourself, which is your constitutional
right, the author and the publisher assume no responsibility for your actions.

Any people depicted in stock imagery provided by Getty Images are
models, and such images are being used for illustrative purposes only.
Certain stock imagery © Getty Images.

Print information available on the last page.

ISBN: 978-1-9822-4237-4 (sc)
ISBN: 978-1-9822-4238-1 (e)

Balboa Press rev. date: 02/27/2020

This book is dedicated to every survivor of addiction, childhood trauma and to those living with Complex PTSD. May my story help you discover and heal that beautiful, broken child within you.

You have suffered long enough. It is time to leave your cage and fly.

# *CONTENTS*

# ACKNOWLEDGEMENTS

I would like to thank the following people who made the writing of this book possible:

My greatest teacher, Dr. A., your wisdom, endless patience, and compassion with me over the years were a light in the darkest time in my life. I can never repay you for showing me how to find and love that little girl.

My husband, for choosing to walk this journey with me. Thank you for being both a mother and father when the darkness and flashbacks consumed my soul. You will never know how much you mean to me and how your love has carried me.

Anne, you have always been the wind beneath my wings, whether you knew it or not.

Lesley, you became much more than my editor. Your kindness, compassion, humour and wisdom made the process of publishing this book so much easier.

My sponsor S, thank you for always being there and encouraging me to do the next right thing. I love you so much.

And my children — my love for you is the reason I fought so hard.

*And the day came when the risk to remain tight in a bud was more painful than the risk it took to blossom.*

**Anaïs Nin**

# CHAPTER
# *ONE*

## GRIEF

I search fearlessly for the gift, for the purpose of my suffering. I have to. I no longer have a choice. There has to be something useful that can come out of the chaos. My pain cannot have been for nothing.

I refuse to let the darkness win, the darkness that for years consumed my soul with its lies and that still lingers to this day, longing to lure me back into its murky shadows of fractured memories — memories I no longer believe are true yet still remain and remind me of the time when I felt shattered into a million pieces.

Instead, I will fan the ember, the Divine spark that dwells within me.

This flame is the source of the burning pyre I am building to consume the sadness, fear, and every distorted memory my childhood abusers instilled in me.

Its light will illuminate the way for her, my beautiful inner child, until she rises like a phoenix from the ashes of her past and soars effortlessly above the cage in which she has been imprisoned for years.

As she begins her freedom from this cage, my heart fills with joy for her. She is no longer a captive, a slave to those fractured memories. She is free to soar anywhere she desires. But as I watch her ascend I notice her fluttering as she struggles to fly with a broken wing. Joy soon turns to grief and this grief feels like a death.

In reality, I am grieving a death. The death of us. I am grieving the death of our childhood and what could have been. I am grieving the loss of our birth family, although many are still living. And sometimes I don't know when, or if, the grief will end because it resides in the very marrow of my bones.

There are times when this grief feels like a bottomless pit of emptiness, of nothingness. I am just a shell, devoid of anything inside me. I am hollow. Then there are other days when grief disguises itself as anger, fear, confusion, and profound sadness. Either way, it feels as if I am crying a lifetime of tears; tears I didn't even know existed in me because for most of my life I have unknowingly repressed every emotion possible. Suppression was how I learned to survive. Don't emote. Pretend. Act as if everything is okay.

I developed this façade during my childhood because I didn't know any better, what child does? Children have an innate need to believe that everything is okay, that there is safety, predictability, and normalcy in their life. Thus, I became a willing participant in my own family's charade. I played my part, and I played it well.

As I continue to heal from my childhood traumas, I am finally allowing myself to cry and rage for that beautiful, freckled-faced, blue-eyed girl who could have been anything she wanted to be, anything at all. But that potential was stolen from her the moment she was born into this world, into her birth family. My abusers stole everything from me. They robbed me of trust — not only in other people, but in myself. They took away happiness and the ability to feel joy. They shattered my innocence, my sense of childhood wonder and awe. My abusers stole my sense of safety, security, and most of all, they stole my emotional wellness. Mental stability. Sanity. Call it what you want, it doesn't matter, they took that too. They made me believe that *I* was the crazy one. They took away my gift of sexuality and turned it into something to be despised, to be ashamed of.

Tragically, these thieves of whom I speak were the very ones who were supposed to have protected, nurtured, and loved me.

Like many survivors of childhood abuse and dysfunction, I've lived most of my life in my head, unsure of what was real, feeling confused, irrevocably broken, and never quite knowing why. In response to this, my brain scanned, analysed, and meticulously tried to unearth every memory from the past to justify my profound sadness and my incessant need to fix the brokenness within me. But what was this brokenness that needed to be fixed?

In my adolescent ignorance, I concluded that it had to be me. It was me who was flawed and damaged and needed to be fixed.

But now I know the truth. I am not broken. I was never broken. They were.

This is a story about a woman. She is not unlike you. She may act and talk just as you do. You may have passed her on the street, seen her at the grocery store. She smiles. She laughs. She plays the game extremely well; everything she does is perfectly executed. No one would ever suspect what is really going on underneath her façade. She hides her terror, confusion, and profound sadness behind one of the many masks she wears. She cannot risk being exposed. Therefore, she unceasingly uses that smile to hide the shame and brokenness that lives and grows and festers within her soul. Pain she has tried to forget about and push away for decades. Pain, she thinks, should no longer matter because she is older now.

But is she? Is she older? Because deep inside, at the very core of who she is, is the little girl she once was. And unbeknownst to the woman, this little girl controls every thought, every action, every feeling she experiences. This little girl obsessively reminds the woman to be afraid and on guard at all times. She demands perfection because anything short of perfection could be disastrous.

This little girl is shattered into a million pieces because she was denied her birthright to be loved and nurtured, to feel safe and protected. She was emotionally abandoned, physically and sexually abused. And when part of her soul died as a result of this, she was buried, entombed within the darkness where her shame became her burial cloth. There was never a funeral or a farewell. She cannot, will not, rest until someone, anyone, rescues her. And because the woman has stifled her cries for help, that little girl still exists, stuck in the mire of darkness, confusion, and fear. The child longs to be validated, to be set free from the chains imposed by others and, more tragically, by the lies she believes about herself.

But how?

How can this possibly happen? The woman does not yet know that, ironically, *she* is the answer, that *she* is the *only* person who can save this little child. Because she doesn't know this, the woman refuses to even acknowledge that the little girl exists. She ignores her pleas for help, day after day, month after month, and year after year. It is the only way she can survive. The truth is too excruciating to believe. Don't think. Don't feel. Pretend. Drink. Drug. Numb. Act as if everything is fine. That is, until the day comes when the child inside her revolts and refuses to be silent a moment longer. This is the story of that woman and that girl.

Me.

I wish I didn't have to write this, but something inside me compels me to. Maybe because the truth needs to be told, maybe because people need to understand the profound and lifelong damage that occurs when a child is emotionally abandoned, neglected, or abused. It isn't fair that this is how a child's life begins and, more important, it is not how an adult's life should end.

I believe that every human being is born with a spark of the Divine within his or her soul. A goodness, a purity, a benevolent presence. This spark is eternal. It can never be extinguished, but it can certainly dim to near blackness depending on the trauma one endures.

A child is born into this world totally pure, magical, and full of wonder and hope. She deserves to feel loved and important, to feel safe, to feel wanted; to know that she is a sacred and beloved child of the universe. To know that no matter what happens, someone, *anyone* will always be there to protect her, even as she grows and matures.

Much of the research throughout the decades supports this, especially John Bowlby's Attachment Theory. He concluded that a strong emotional and physical attachment to at least one parent is *absolutely essential* to a person's development. But sadly, many parents or caretakers are unable to fulfil this. Unconditional love, acceptance, and security is not a given for many children. As a result, this critical developmental need is unmet. Many survivors of childhood abuse and/or neglect walk through life feeling that something is inherently wrong, irrevocably broken and defective within *them*. Yet they cannot quite understand the cause, the reason for such soul-crushing shame. Their spark dims, hidden beneath layers of pain. This is precisely what happened to me.

I truly thought I had a normal childhood, but now, from an adult's perspective, I see it was far from normal. There were secrets.

Abuse. Dysfunction. Fractured memories. And because of this, deep inside my being I knew something was not quite right. A war constantly raged in my mind. The relentless obsession to understand and figure out this war led to despair and helplessness. I reasoned that if I figured it out, I would be able to fix it — the unworthiness, sadness, shame, and fear that I felt every single day of my life.

I have since learned the truth, however: yes, there was a war within me, but I did not start this war.

I am sure as hell going to end it though.

I am also compelled to write this book for other reasons. First, I have been graced with the gift of healing from Complex-PTSD and alcoholism. Sadly, from my contact with those of a similar fate, I know not every victim of abuse receives these gifts. Not only do they have limited access to the resources needed to understand and process their trauma, they do not believe they have the ability to heal from this disorder. Without this belief, recovery just isn't possible. So I feel I have an obligation. I need to share my story and offer hope to others, for I too once believed I would never be able to put the pieces of my soul back together. Instead, I unwillingly accepted that this was how I was destined to spend my days on this earth. I need to share how I began the arduous process of believing and trusting in *my own* ability to heal myself.

Finally, and perhaps most significantly, I write this for **HER**, the little girl in me who never had a voice and for decades was a prisoner to fear. Her voice was silenced a long time ago, before she even uttered her first word. There are so many things I need to tell her, so many things I want her to know and understand. More important, there are so many things about her that I want others to know because I recognize that she is not the only one who has lived through this kind of soul death. There are still countless men and women who do not believe recovery from childhood trauma is possible. It is possible. Paradoxically, *she,* that beautiful little girl in me whom I despised for most of my existence, was the one who showed me how to heal. For decades I obsessively searched for the answer *outside* of myself. I didn't find the answer in any of the self-help books I read. I didn't find it through the countless years of psychotherapy or through abusing alcohol and drugs. Nor did I find it in an organized religion. Those things only offered me insight and at times helped ease the pain. Instead, I found the answer to my inexplicable suffering deep down inside, in my soul where that little girl still lived, terrified and alone.

And this is where everyone's answer lies.

I want *her* voice, which was silenced for decades, to be the voice of hope for those who are still too afraid or ashamed to look deep within themselves, where their wounded child lives. This child is waiting to be recognized, to be noticed. She is waiting for her cries to be heard and validated. She has been waiting endlessly to be held, hugged, and comforted. And she is waiting to hear the truth — that she is innocent, pure, whole, and blameless.

This book recounts how I was able to reach my own wounded inner child after decades of repression and self-hatred. When I finally acknowledged her, we were able to start a relationship. Slowly she began to trust me, to expose her pain and vulnerabilities. It was only then that I discovered the nightmare she had endured because of the actions of the adults around her and the coping mechanisms she developed to survive those atrocities. I learned to dialogue with her and through this process, she began to heal. And in turn, I began to heal. This led to the discovery of a spirituality and a truth within me that I never knew existed.

# CHAPTER
# *TWO*

## WHAT IS C-PTSD?

I have Complex-PTSD. As the name suggests, Complex-PTSD (C-PTSD) is more complicated than Post Traumatic Stress Disorder (PTSD). PTSD is a mental health condition that results from experiencing or witnessing a terrifying event. Complex PTSD, however, develops in response to *repeated and/or prolonged* trauma, often starting in childhood. My trauma psychiatrist shared with me that C-PTSD does not only come from ongoing physical and sexual abuse, it can also result from emotional neglect and abandonment.

Complex-PTSD is not yet fully recognized in the DSM,[1] the medical manual that contains the criteria used for diagnosing mental disorders. I find this both distressing and surprising because on my healing journey I have met many people whom I believe would meet the criteria for this.

C-PTSD makes the brain feel ravaged, as if it is involved in a war. Its neurons are firing endlessly in the wrong direction. It does

---

[1] *Diagnostic and Statistical Manual of Mental Disorders*

not know which side it should fight for. Should it fight with its past, with all the coping mechanisms it developed and which were needed to protect itself from the enemies? Or should it fight on the side of the present, fearlessly face the past by walking across the battlefield and surrendering its (no longer useful) coping mechanisms? You would think the decision would be easy, but I can assure you it is brutal. This has been the most difficult challenge I have had to face in recovery.

The brain does not want to give up its artillery — those coping mechanisms that an abused child or adolescent develops and uses to survive the war that raged around her. She had to be hypervigilant and on guard every minute. She needed to outsmart her enemies, to predict their moves, in order to avoid another conflict, another abuse, another assault. These coping mechanisms saved her life — how can she possibly give them up now?

Eventually, the child grows, passes through adolescence and matures into adulthood. The assault, the battle, is long over. Perhaps decades have passed. It is understandably assumed that the adult is now enjoying a time of peace.

But to an adult with unresolved childhood trauma, there is no resolution to the internal conflict, no reconciliation. The traumatic memories and the relentless coping mechanisms of this long-ago battle remain stuck, trapped deep within the brain; imprinted and engraved. They are next to impossible to erase.

A wounded warrior has been abandoned, forgotten, and left behind. Therefore, the brain will repudiate any agreement, any discussion about a possible cease-fire. It believes it still needs to protect this forgotten warrior.

But who is the wounded warrior and where is she?

It is the inner child.

She remains hidden, terrified, and camouflaged in the muddied darkness of her soul. She is tangled up in the barbed wires of her mind. She cannot comprehend why you, the adult, won't acknowledge her, why you have buried and forgotten about her.

This inner child has been knocking on the door of your subconscious for years, but you have not dared answer that knock. You haven't wanted to think or be reminded about the pain or the traumatic memories of your past. You might even try to silence her pleas by numbing yourself with whatever substance you can find.

Make no mistake, that child will continue banging until you relent. But even then, when you finally risk unbolting that lock, she will not trust you. She may see *you* as the enemy. If you are like me, you were the one who unknowingly abandoned and buried her all those years ago. And that child remains exactly as you left her with all her unresolved layers of pain, fear, confusion and sadness. Therefore, you will need to be patient with her. You need to be gentle, understanding, compassionate — all the things the adults in your childhood were not. And you will find that the only thing she desires is the healing balm of *your* love.

# CHAPTER THREE

## ACCEPTANCE

I have multiple childhood and adolescent traumas, ranging from sexual and physical abuse to emotional neglect. This has taken me years to acknowledge, let alone accept.

It is only now, after years of intense trauma therapy, that I understand what really transpired and the effect it had on my still developing psyche. This understanding, as well as a faith in something bigger than myself, have assisted in the acceptance that I am not bad, broken, or crazy the way my mind repeatedly told me I was.

I was traumatized. Period.

Initially, my acceptance of this diagnosis was very difficult for three reasons.

First, I did not want to think badly of my abusers because they were members of both my immediate and extended family. It was easier for me to blame myself for everything that happened than to admit that my own family had in any way harmed me. It was easier to push away and minimize — even rationalize — the memory of my favourite uncle taking advantage of me when I was a child and sexually abusing me than to confront him or tell anyone. I was too afraid, and too young to understand that what he'd done was wrong.

Second, acceptance of C-PTSD means that for *decades* I have had my entire life story wrong. Backwards. Completely skewed. My initial traumas happened during my childhood and adolescence. Sadly, when the memories resurfaced, they were processed through uninformed, childish, and ignorant eyes and, tragically, I constructed and believed *my own version* of the events. The story was completely distorted. At the time, I never discussed it with a single person and so had no one to tell me otherwise, to tell me how wrong I was to blame myself.

It was this distortion of the events that caused me to experience what is known as *secondary trauma*. Secondary trauma is the emotional response (like PTSD) an individual experiences when she witnesses or hears a narrative or a "vivid recounting from a survivor" of a traumatic event.

And who was the narrator in the story of my abuses? It was me. Not an adult, but an adolescent girl without any understanding of the facts.

How could I possibly have known how to process my past any differently than I did back then? I had no one in my life to tell me how wrong my perception was. I've learned that every event a person experiences is processed through the mind's age at the time the event happened. Thus, when the memories came back, my young mind coloured my story with untruths and misconceptions. In *my* story, my abusers were innocent and I was the villain. I was the bad girl. Immoral. And I was convinced that because of this, I was going to hell. Literally.

The symptoms and losses I experienced from this secondary trauma have been immeasurable. I despise that I have to accept this, it is so unfair. How do I accept that I traumatized *myself* because of what *they* did and because of my misperception of it? How do I accept having lost the best years, the best decades, of my life? I can never get those years back. My childhood innocence was taken from me, as was my adolescence. Sometimes I become lost just watching young children at play. I hear their laughter. I can actually feel their joy. I observe their wonder and curiosity about anything and everything. They are so unafraid, so beautiful and innocent. Their existence is just effortless. I didn't get that. I will never experience that. I was always afraid. My childhood innocence was torn right out of my nine-year old soul the second my sexual abuse occurred. How do I accept this? I will never know what it feels like to be just a regular kid.

I lost the ability to trust and believe — and not just other people, but myself. To this day, I struggle with trust, especially trusting that I am whole and emotionally well. I constantly have to be reminded by loved ones and my doctor that I am well and that it is okay to be well. I live in terror of going back to that place of darkness and suffering, and yet ironically feel uncomfortable in the light because it is so foreign to me.

Like many survivors of childhood sexual abuse, I also lost the beautiful gift of sexuality and intimacy. The loss of this gift is far reaching and not only affects me, it affects my husband as well. Intimacy, even with the man I love and adore, makes me feel completely uncomfortable. It is difficult to open up sexually because my mind is often on my trauma. I feel raw. Vulnerable. Exposed. Ashamed.

Finally (and perhaps most tragically) I lost my emotional wellness as a result of toxic shame, flashbacks, and maladaptive coping mechanisms. Although I am now so much better at managing my flashbacks, the initial panic that accompanies them can be paralysing. Almost automatically, I often become caught up in catastrophizing and the "what ifs"...what if I get stuck *eternally* in a flashback, what if I go back to the time when I actually believed in all the lies, what if I can't let go of old maladaptive coping mechanisms? My God, what if I never get better? What if this is my life forever? What if I remain stuck in the prison of my own mind and its memories.

For years, I thought I suffered from mental illness and I accepted this label without question. I have since learned that symptoms of C-PTSD can mimic or co-exist with other forms of mental illness. I suffered from feelings of intense shame, emotional dysregulation, crippling anxiety, depression, and flashbacks. I had no knowledge of what was happening to me, so I sought answers from every kind of doctor imaginable. From the age of twenty, I have been diagnosed with everything from major depression, to severe anxiety, to obsessive compulsive disorder (OCD). And because of this, the treatments I received only focused on those specific mental illnesses. My past seemed to be completely irrelevant. No one who treated me ever took it into account, or even asked about it. And I, still believing I was to blame for my problems, did not consider it either. I also assumed that because it occurred in childhood, it no longer mattered.

Over the years I was given medication after medication to try to alleviate the internal chaos I was experiencing. I am very grateful I had the courage to take these medications despite the fear and the stigma attached to taking any drug for "mental illness." For me, medication was necessary. It definitely helped and calmed me down to a point where I could function and begin to accurately process my trauma.

I have also spent countless hours and money on therapy. I read every self-help and new age book available. But still, the chaos remained. It was as if there was a block somewhere deep in my brain that was preventing me, *forbidding* me, to understand what was really going on in my mind.

The shame, the feeling of craziness, confusion, and sadness would never go away. They became my daily companions and yet remained complete strangers by never allowing me to fully understand the reason for their presence. They woke with me in the mornings and lay beside me at night. I despised them and therefore hated who I was. And so, that war within me began to rage. Decades of self-blame and self-hate taunted me and told me I would never get over it; I would never understand and be able to heal from this inexplicable pain; I was unworthy of any kind of happiness. In my darkest times, my companions would whisper, "Why bother? Give up. No one will ever love or help you. You're stuck with us forever."

There were many times I wanted to — and almost did — give up. I had yet to discover that what I was suffering from was C-PTSD from childhood abuses, and that what I had been experiencing all this time were its symptoms.

Thankfully, that beautiful little girl inside me somehow knew better than I did. There were so many times I wanted to quit trying to get well, to get better. Because I had no understanding of the causes for it, and no one to share it with, the battle was exhausting and felt futile. There were days when I woke in the morning and thought, I just can't fight anymore.

She, on the other hand, was resilient — a warrior. And she was always singlehandedly battling the internal warfare. Today, I believe that it was SHE who subconsciously encouraged me to keep fighting no matter how I felt. Somehow, she let me know that somewhere there was hope, that on the other side of the darkness, there had to be light. That on the other side of this profound despair, there had to be joy. That this hell I was living in was not based on any kind of reality.

And so, she persevered until I could acknowledge her and what had been our truth for decades. I am eternally grateful that she never quit. Had she done so, I would not have the beautiful life I have today. I wouldn't have my beautiful children who are without a doubt the most precious gifts I have ever received. Not every day is perfect, but it is far more manageable than it once was. Today I have hope things will only get better because I have already healed from so much of the pain and shame that I was *convinced* I would *never* let go of. And this is the hope that I want to offer to you.

Most important, if it weren't for her tenacity and determination, I never would have discovered that a beautiful truth, a benevolent presence lay unknowingly within me, patiently waiting to be discovered if I was brave enough to search for it. This truth, this benevolent presence that cannot adequately be described with words, was hidden beneath my countless layers of pain and traumas. But I now believe that it has *always* been there, I was just blocked from acknowledging it.

This magnificent truth, this knowing who I *really* am, has the ability to set me free from the bondage of my suffering *if* I allow it to. It is the place I now instinctively go to when I am afraid or symptomatic. When I do so, I find a peace and comfort that I have never before experienced. It envelops me in its arms and reassures me that all is well and I need not fight anymore. I am safe. I am protected. And that not only am I loved beyond any human understanding, *I am love.* I am not my suffering or my trauma. Those were just horrible experiences. I am love. I am pure. I am good. I am light.

Therefore, I can never quit on her, my inner child. I will never quit on her, *ever.* I will always be there for her when she is in a flashback or is symptomatic. Instead of despairing, panicking, or repressing the intense emotions and trauma thoughts as I have always done (and still occasionally do), I am now learning to calmly go to her, sit and talk her through whatever it is she is experiencing. I remind her that what she is feeling is just a flashback — it is a *re-experiencing, a re-feeling* of her original and secondary trauma. That's all. *It is only a memory of those past events.* I remind her that she is not back in that terrifying and confusing place. She is no longer that child, alone and helpless. I am now her parent, her protector, and her encourager. I remind her that she has already survived the war and that the war no longer exists except in her memory.

There are times when I truly believe that the fallout from my traumas, especially my secondary trauma, are far worse than the actual abuses I endured as a child. I have hated, despised C-PTSD and its brutal symptoms and, therefore, have hated parts of me. As I continue to heal, and as I have grown to love my inner child, I now see what this hatred implies. If I hate my C-PTSD and its symptoms, am I not, in turn, hating *her*, my inner child? Am I not hating the child who actually *went through and somehow survived* the abuses? The one who was intelligent and clever enough to come up with these coping mechanisms *to survive*?

No. I can't and I won't do that. I will no longer hate this disorder because I absolutely refuse to hate any part of her. She is a miracle. A survivor. A warrior. She has been through enough hatred in this lifetime.

She didn't cause my C-PTSD, my abusers did. *They* caused me, an innocent adolescent, to develop coping mechanisms — coping mechanisms that included hypervigilance, OCD/intrusive thinking, questioning and needing answers and certainty in order to be prepared for any catastrophe that might befall me. My incessant need to know and understand things helped my mind dodge any potential danger that could be lurking in the shadows. These coping mechanisms were brilliant at the time and served me well. As an adult however, they became maladaptive because there was no longer a reason or use for them. It was completely safe for me to disarm. But my traumatized brain didn't know that yet. It had yet to uncover the truth and was still in survival mode.

These coping mechanisms still remain but are definitely dissipating, mainly because I have finally *accepted the fact* that they are structurally part of my brain. I do not possess the power to change how my brain developed. Instead, I remind myself that *I wasn't born* with these maladaptive behaviours and therefore, they are not part of who I really am. I would *never* have created or needed them if it weren't for my abusers. So who is to blame for them? Who do they really belong to? To me or to them?

I am learning, albeit slowly, to accept that my mind functions the way it does and is *perfectly normal* for what I have been through. I have been repeatedly reminded that my thinking is absolutely normal for the abnormal situation I grew up in. This knowledge helps me a lot. As abused children, our still developing minds created a certain way of thinking to survive the unimaginable, the incomprehensible.

Accepting this remains one of the biggest challenges I have faced thus far and it remains my greatest sadness. I don't like the way I think or the way I process information. It is always tainted in some way with my past. I want my brain to be "normal." I often stare at people and wonder what it would it be like to have a brain that functions the way it is *supposed* to, without the interference of intruding trauma thoughts or old coping mechanisms. I imagine it would feel so freeing and so wonderful. I will never know what that is like.

The sadness occurs because I know I have missed out on some of life's greatest moments because I am only "partially present" most of the time. Even today, there still remains an urge, a need to scan the battlefield for what problem may arise.

But, as the years passed, I've tried not to participate in the delusion of believing I can ever (or should) think the way a "normal" adult does…whatever that means.

What is normal anyway?

Initially, this was my goal. I always had this weird belief that I could not be happy until my mind was perfectly normal and trauma free. I truly believed that this was a possibility and so I worked tirelessly toward trying to accomplish this. I have spent so much mental energy trying to control the uncontrollable — the memories and the traumatic thoughts. They cannot be erased. They will always be there. They are part of me. Upon reflection, I am repeating the cycle of repression, just in a different way; a different re-enactment of my past behaviour.

As a child, it was: be perfect, Dad will be happy, you will be happy.

As an adolescent, it was: be perfect, God will be happy, you will be happy. Today it has morphed into, think perfect, you will be happy. Perfectionism, however it presents itself, is closely linked with childhood abuse. Children believe that if they just try harder, if they become the perfect son or daughter, perhaps they will receive that parental love and acceptance they so desperately crave. Perhaps they will be spared abuse from their parent. Perfectionism was one of my coping mechanisms. I was always desperately trying to be what I thought other people wanted me to be and thus, I never became my authentic self.

Until now.

Trauma's coping mechanisms are insidious; they disguise themselves in many ways but their roots will never change. Thankfully, because I am now aware of their origins, the how and why they began, that death grip feeling of anxiety I used to have when they occurred is gone. Now the feeling is more of frustration and an ache that they still linger. It is my hope that with time and understanding, my inner child will feel safe enough to totally let go of this old habit.

I will never be perfect in any way, shape, or form. Perfection is just an old childhood belief I developed to try to keep myself safe and have people love and accept me.

I do not possess the power to unravel the thinking patterns my brain formed to protect me. I have finally surrendered this need, and with surrender comes the painful process of acceptance — acceptance of all the losses I experienced.

Today, I name the emotion or the coping mechanism I am experiencing and the reason for it, because there is *always* a reason, a root cause. I quiet my mind and I go to her, my inner child. In my mind, we sit together and chat about why she is afraid and what she is experiencing. I remind her *why* she is experiencing it. I always reiterate the truth of what really happened to her so that knowledge becomes solidified. Then we let go of as much emotion and old beliefs as we can for that moment. I never force her to do anything before she is ready.

The point is, I no longer ignore her or repress the feeling. I always answer her cries. In answering her cries, she begins to trust me more, and in response I begin to trust myself more.

Today, I am choosing to see my trauma as the strongest part of who I am, because in reality it represents the strength, resilience, and courage of the child I once was. *A child.*

But I do grieve for her. I grieve that she continues to sometimes experience the symptoms of C-PTSD because of the irresponsible actions of adults. I grieve because she was so young and didn't understand what was happening to her. I grieve that when the memories resurfaced, she viewed them not through the eyes of a mature adult, but through the eyes of a broken and vulnerable adolescent and, therefore, understood the entire story completely wrong. To me, this is the profound tragedy of this entire mess because the consequences were catastrophic.

It saddens me that she unknowingly had to come up with those coping mechanisms just to survive the chaos she was living in. What child should ever have to come up with coping mechanisms? And today, I am *finally allowing* myself to feel and to grieve. I sob whenever I need to. I journal. I hug my dog. I try and let the impenetrable fortress I built around myself break down just a little bit so I can let in those who love me.

And every single day, I talk to her.

When I started doing this, I thought maybe it was abnormal. When I talked to my trauma doctor about it, he reassured me that many survivors of childhood trauma who re-connect with their inner child do this. Dialoguing is completely normal. It offers her comfort and security. It allows me the opportunity to re-parent her in the way she needed to be but never was.

Re-parenting is self explanatory. My adult self (along with my newfound knowledge) metaphorically "goes back" and fulfils all of my inner child's emotional needs that were never met. I get to be the parent that she needed while she was growing up. I get to nurture and love her. I empathize with her. I soothe her when she needs it. I remind her there is no need, as she once believed, to worry, obsess, or catastrophize.

There are still times when I feel like she is in the driver's seat and running the show, so to speak. Her emotions, questions, and her "what ifs" are overwhelming. It is during these times, my re-parenting strategies change. I have to be firm with her. I sometimes tell her to just stop with the chaos. I remind her that I love her but I am the adult and therefore in charge, not her. I believe this builds trust, boundaries, and a belief in each-other.

This re-parenting and the ensuing relationship with my inner child is absolutely and *without a doubt* the piece that most helped me to exponentially heal. And it is my belief that *this is the piece* that will heal most survivors of childhood or adolescent trauma. *This is the answer.*

Sometimes I rage but it is no longer ever directed at her. My anger is now directed at the adults in my childhood who did nothing to nurture, protect me, or help create even a semblance of self-love or self-worth within me. That was their job. It is every parent's job. I rage that a religious institution could instil such fear into a child that she feels she is unworthy of joy or of life itself because any human mistake she makes is unacceptable — a sin. I rage that these institutions teach that our Creator is cruel and vengeful, instead of compassionate, loving, and kind. I rage that I had no one to help me with this life altering misunderstanding of my past, a misunderstanding that I carried my whole life.

I truly believe that after being repressed for decades, all my beautiful little girl wanted was an explanation, a justification for this war that continued to consume her despite the cease-fire. That's all. She desperately wanted *just one* person to talk to her, to explain what was happening and why it was happening. One person to give her permission to finally feel and release all the emotions and fears she was clinging to so that she could walk out of that self-imposed prison. And ultimately, to have enough courage to walk right over the enemy lines, right up to her uncle, her family, to that man-made religion and give all of it, all of the pain and suffering, back to them. The original owners. The initiators. The instigators.

CHAPTER
# FOUR

## WHO ARE WE REALLY?

C hildhood abuse and neglect completely robs a person of her identity. Critical milestones in emotional development are not met. Because of this, I spent my childhood feeling completely different from other children. I became an observer, watching how they interacted with each other and not understanding why I couldn't be like them. As I grew older, my world felt tilted. Off balance. Fuzzy. It was difficult to concentrate because I was so busy existing in a state of hypervigilance. All my energies were devoted to becoming this perfect person in order to protect myself and my emotional wellbeing. I had no time to think about who I might become, what dreams I might want to fulfil. I was completely inauthentic. Empty. Confused.

My therapist recently suggested that it might be wise for me to take some time off to find out who I "authentically" am without my traumas. What was frightening about this is that it made me realize I have no idea who I am. I have always lived through labels: a daughter, sister, mom, educator, wife, and as the years marched on these labels became darker and more oppressive —alcoholic, fuck-up, mental case.

Who am I without these labels? Who is *anybody* really?

I didn't know what or who I was before my traumas and I certainly had no clue when I started this journey. Just trying to survive what I perceived was "normal" is all I have ever known. So it was daunting when I was challenged to take a break from my daily routine and just sit with my thoughts. Sitting with my thoughts and feelings was the last thing I wanted to do. I had always run away from them, buried them. My thoughts were always focused on some aspect of my traumas and to suggest I just "sit with them" felt like a death sentence. Attempting to discover my authentic self also made me wonder, who would I be if I were born into a different family? Who would I be if I hadn't been abused? What talents might I have that were never nurtured? Could I have been a great painter? A gifted musician? Would I have travelled the world had I not been so afraid and anxious all the time? Would I have had a different career? Married someone else? Had more children? No children? The possibilities could be endless.

One thing I am sure of is that I will never know what life that girl inside me might have had if she had been born into a different family. That girl is dead. She was buried a long time ago with whatever dreams she may have carried in her heart, dreams I will never know about. She died the moment she was born into her family. Any laughter and joy she may have experienced in her childhood died. Self-confidence and love died. Self-worth died. Her basic trust in human beings died. And her death gave birth to a person who merely existed. Existing only to undo and work out the destruction caused by other people.

I heeded my doctor's advice and took a leave of absence from work. It was the only way I could actually sit still and be with myself. I would force myself to stop running from my feelings by keeping insanely busy; I would instead just sit with them. Because my children would be at school, I knew there would be no one at home during this period who could distract me or prevent me from putting on one of many masks. I would just do what my intuition guided me to do. I reasoned that if I did have an overwhelming symptom, feeling, or trauma thought, I could safely express the energy behind it because there wouldn't be any witnesses to a potential meltdown. And there were a lot of meltdowns.

The first few weeks were horrible. The trauma thoughts and fears beckoned me to re-enlist in my army of one and return to the war zone. My memories and fears wanted me back in those trenches and tried to convince me I needed that armour of self-protection — my hypervigilance and my old coping mechanisms. But I refused to be recruited again. I would not go down the trauma vortex again.

Instead, I finally allowed myself to think and feel everything without breaking down, becoming unhinged, and then repressing it as I had done in the past. Instead, I released the repressed energy by allowing myself to sob non-stop. Sometimes I raged and screamed at the top of my lungs while punching pillows or the couch. There were times I just held my dog or slept the entire day. I did whatever it was I felt I was being guided to do. There was no agenda or manual for what I was supposed to do.

My main outlet, though, became writing. I started journaling, and what I wrote was primal, raw, and came straight from my soul. I wrote as if no one would ever read my words. I unleashed years of feelings and emotions. I wrote to myself. I wrote to my abusers. I wrote to my alcoholism. I wrote to my inner child. My suffering had initially expressed itself in thoughts, thoughts that tormented me. Soon, these thoughts became words. These words became my voice, the voice I had buried long ago. I filled notebook after notebook, and I would burn them when I was done because the idea of anyone finding them terrified me. No one except a victim of childhood abuse would understand them.

My writing became a healing tool and helped me make sense of the madness, that war that remained in my soul. It helped me put the puzzle pieces of my fractured mind on a table and then arrange them until they began to form a coherent picture, an understanding.

But still, that question my doctor had posed remained. *Who am I?* I thought about this a lot. I wonder how many people on this earth actually take the time out of the madness of this world to ponder that question.

Are we just human beings? Are we spiritual beings? Or are we spiritual beings having a human experience? What does spirit or soul even mean?

It occurred to me that in order to even try to answer this question, I had to return to the very beginning of my existence and start again. I needed to go back to when I first came into existence on this planet and my beliefs about how that happened. And what I believe is that I was a spark of the divine. Everyone is.

I was part of a whole, like a drop in an ocean or a beam from the sun. *I was part of a Source. And that Source was benevolent and beautiful.*

I was perfect. Innocent. Sane. I was unblemished. Pure. Full of possibilities. Shame-free.

If I am born with a tiny spark of the Divine in me, does this Divine, Source, Creator, Christ, Unconditional Love, Energy — whatever its name is — actually *live inside me*? And if it lives inside me, am I not Divine too? With this knowledge and belief, I can be anything and face any challenge. I have Divine Light *living* right inside me, guiding me to do the next right thing for my highest good, my soul's purpose....

Imagine.

Think about it.

This idea really resonated with me and thus began my journey of rediscovering my spirit and my soul.

To remind myself that this is who I truly am, always was and always will be, I taped a picture of me as a newborn baby on my bathroom mirror. All I see when I gaze at that face is purity and innocence with an entire life ahead of her. A perfect soul experiencing life. A life without abuse, a life without trauma. *A part of the Source, the Divine.*

This is who we all were before the layers of trauma darkened our light. Before the trauma shattered our souls and made us feel it was impossible to discover our truth. Before we were made to believe in the deception and lies we told ourselves. Before we were unceasingly and hopelessly suspended between the past and the present, not understanding which tense we belonged in. Before the thieves, our abusers, nearly robbed us of everything we might have become.

Now, on waking each morning, I try to breathe in and welcome my divinity, that newborn baby's purity and light. I remind myself that the truth lies within my heart, *not my head.* My head only contains the inaccurate, *imprinted* traumatic memories, the lies I once believed about my trauma. My head, my mind is only the *human* part of me. When I am gone from this earth, so will those memories be gone. My heart, however, embraces the Divine, which is eternal. It contains my soul, my spirit, and the *truth. This part* will live forever.

When the enemy in my mind tries to engage me in its battle of lies and fear, I pause and focus on the area around my heart where I believe my soul and my little girl lives. I allow my heart's knowledge and divinity to comfort her until every cell feels immersed in light. The knowingness comes that THIS is who I truly am: pure Divine light, safe and protected. This is who we *all* are.

When I open my eyes, the enemy and its lies has retreated. It has lost a little more of its power over me. The more I practice this, the stronger my light, my inner truth becomes.

# CHAPTER
# *FIVE*

## REPRESSION

As a teenager, I unknowingly repressed my childhood abuse and trauma. Perhaps it was because I had my "other family" at my best friend's home, a safe, loving environment. Anne and I met when we were thirteen. She remains my best friend to this day. She comes from a huge, loving European family. I was immediately welcomed into her family and treated with enormous kindness by everyone. There was a different energy in that house. Sure, there were disagreements, but none that would end in violence or isolation. I felt envious of the invisible bond they all seemed to share, but also very grateful they considered me their adopted daughter. In my ignorance, when I compared her family to mine, I assumed her family must simply be unique. As I have walked this road of recovery, I now know her family wasn't all that unusual – it was MY family that was.

Perhaps I repressed my trauma because I didn't know or understand that what had been happening to me was abuse. I have learned that, like me, many abused children believe that what is

31

happening to them is normal. Because their brains are not fully formed, and because their experience in the world is limited, they have no measuring stick for what is "normal." What they know and are familiar with is normal for *them*. Perhaps my brain had already gone into survival mode and would not allow me to comprehend the enormity and devastation of what was occurring. It was only when I looked at my past through *adult eyes* that I began to see that something was wrong. Very wrong.

Tragically, I believe I repressed my past because a false belief had been growing and festering deep within me. I was internalizing all the messages that surrounded me. Subconsciously I believed what my abusers were insidiously instilling in me: that I was unworthy, broken, unimportant. Because these messages lay deep within my childhood subconscious, they were difficult to understand and dismiss.

Yet.

Whatever the reason for this repression, I miraculously managed to graduate from high school. I applied to different universities and was accepted into one that required me to move away from home. I remember being excited about this new adventure, thinking it might be a new beginning. But I was also dreading it because I was leaving the security of the one person I knew who loved me unconditionally, Anne.

I found a room in a house close to the university's campus. As the day to leave approached, I started to panic. I wasn't sure if leaving my home and the safety of Anne had been the right decision.

The day I was to go arrived. My dad was driving me there. Neither my mother nor my sisters came, but Anne did. I don't recall any hugs of encouragement, excitement, or emotion from my family when I left. Maybe I'm wrong. What I do remember is my father dropping me off, bringing my things up to my new room, and saying a quick goodbye.

I was a teenager leaving home for the first time and I was scared. I wished my dad had stayed longer, helped me unpack and chatted with me. I wished my mother had come along and offered me some words of wisdom. I wished they'd told me how proud they were that I had taken this massive step of moving away from home and beginning university. Most of all, I really wished they'd said they were going to miss me.

In retrospect, perhaps all these wishes would have come to pass had I spoken up. Maybe I should have told them how I was feeling, that I was afraid and needed their support. But I didn't. I never spoke up about anything. Somewhere along the way in my young life, I had lost my voice. I never felt safe telling them, telling anyone, what I wanted, how I was feeling, or what I *needed*. I felt that I had no right to do so and the following stories will illustrate why this happened.

I wish I could go back in time and sit with that scared teenager, leaving home for the first time. I wish I could have nurtured and loved her. I wish I could have held her and said,

*Oh my sweet girl, how frightened you must be.*

*I'm so sorry that no one seems to care that you're leaving home.*

*You must feel so unloved and unimportant.*

*Your entire family should be here, showing interest in where you're moving to.*

*I know you want their reassurance that you'll be okay and that everything will be fine.*

*I want you to know that* I *think what you're doing is very brave.*

*I'm so proud of you for finishing high school and pushing through your adolescence, despite everything you've been through.*

*You've been so strong for so long, honey.*

*You have unknowingly lived through so much pain and I know you're getting tired.*

*I'm right here, my love. Can you feel me?*

*I'm not ever going to leave you.*

*We will crawl into your bed together at night when you are alone, in this unfamiliar, strange house with these people you don't even know.*

*I will wrap my arms around you and hold you and keep you safe.*

*You can tell me all your fears, worries, and dreams.*
*You're so innocent and beautiful.*
*I love you more than you can imagine.*
*You are going to be okay.*

But I wasn't okay. My first year of university was disastrous. Terrified does not even begin to describe how I felt. I put every ounce of my energy into my classes and did well academically, but psychologically and socially I was starting to break, to crack apart. I couldn't find my place in that world. I felt unworthy. Different. Socially awkward. The students seemed so carefree and happy. It was weird. This marked the beginning of isolating myself. I started to avoid people, especially males. These attractive young students would call on me to hang out and I would hide and choose not to answer the door.

Why would I do that? That should have been a massive red flag for me, but I was totally oblivious to why I was behaving the way I was.

Part of me wanted so desperately to have an intimate connection with one of these guys but another unknown, hidden part of my being was screaming, "Danger!! You can't go there. They might find out what you're hiding."

I was so young, inexperienced and naïve. I couldn't understand what was driving these feelings of unworthiness. I began to experience anxiety. I hated being away from home and wanted to go back and be surrounded by what I knew was "my normal." I craved the safety and security of my friendship with Anne.

I made the decision to finish that year and transfer to a school where I could live at home again. At first, I was relieved to be home, to be where things were familiar and where I assumed I would be happy again. But I quickly became inexplicably sad. I had witnessed another way — a way of normal, carefree, and contented adolescence and it had awakened an internal conflict in me.

I was beginning to be attacked psychologically. I now know these attacks were really emotional flashbacks. My subconscious had been awakened and was assaulting me with the shame-based messages I had absorbed when I was younger and being abused.

*You're worthless.*

*You're bad.*

*You will never be happy like those kids at university.*

I had no idea why I was feeling like this and it was terrifying. I would be fine one minute and then have an overwhelming sense of fear and sadness the next.

The enemy was preparing to use its greatest assault weapon against me: my own mind with all its distorted, inaccurate memories and beliefs. Beliefs that were initially formed in a child's mind, from an abused adolescent's perspective. Memories that I had repressed and had become fractured and skewed because they'd been buried for so long. These memories, when they resurfaced, were so disturbing to my already fragile adolescent mind that they caused me to experience yet *another* trauma, my secondary trauma. To this day, I believe the impact from my secondary trauma far outweighed any primary abuse I endured as a child.

Brene Brown, one of my favorite authors and leading researchers on the topic of shame, wrote, "Sometimes the most dangerous thing for kids is the silence that allows them to construct their own stories — stories that almost always cast them as alone and unworthy of love and belonging."

When I read this, it was as if she was talking about me. I'd constructed my version of the story of my past and I'd done so in total silence. I was the writer, the editor, and the publisher of this horrific tale. Brown further states that shame needs three things to exponentially grow: silence, secrecy, and judgement. And I did just that. I kept my abuses a secret, I shared them with no one, and then I judged myself.

I remember my initial reaction to the memories was complete disbelief. But as the days turned to weeks and my silence continued, I started to experience intense shame, fear, hypervigilance, and paranoia about the possibility that people might find out what happened to me and what I had done in response. These became my most prominent C-PTSD symptoms and were hard-wired and cemented into my still young brain. In fact, this secondary trauma was so intense and so severe, that it made me believe I was totally losing my mind and going crazy.

Can you supress impending madness?

Can you supress crazy?

You can if you're clever enough.

And I was. And I did.

This could very well have been the end of my story. The headline of the newspaper article might have read, "Teenage Girl Dies by Suicide, Reason Unknown, 'She Seemed So Happy.'"

I became so immersed in toxic shame from my memories that I could have very well killed myself. Sometimes I am surprised I didn't. Many victims do. Others remain stuck in the darkness of their shame and flashbacks. They might use alcohol or other addictions to numb their pain. And others choose never, ever to go back there and revisit the horrific memories of their abuse.

I have been told by experts in the field of childhood trauma that I am the anomaly. I didn't kill myself. Furthermore, I accomplished things that most victims of childhood trauma do not. I finished my university degree. I got married. I had children. But all these things came at a massive price. What price did I pay? I paid for this by completely self abandoning and loosing any authentic connection I had with myself and others. I absolutely refused to acknowledge or listen to that child and that teenager within me and the memories they carried.

I paid the price with the loss of emotional wellness.

I pretended.

I became a perfectionist.

I reasoned that if I did all the things that "normal" individuals do, maybe people wouldn't discover the secret I was hiding. Maybe they would never find out the shame and despair I dealt with every day, and perhaps they wouldn't find out what had happened to me and what I had done.

My performance was Oscar worthy.

No one would ever guess at the extraordinary amount of fear, sadness, and shame I was trying to suppress and yet was totally immersed in. Not even my husband, the man I loved and adored, had a clue as to how my soul was shattering and how crazy I thought I myself to be. I thought by not sharing what had happened to me, I was protecting him. I wanted him to be happy and continue with on with his life. I began building that wall, that impenetrable fortress around myself, brick by brick, year by year. I started pushing him farther and farther away.

Some people might say I was just being deceitful. It is much more complicated than that. My entire being was screaming out to be helped, to be saved from this impending sense of doom. But how could I share my past, my pain, and my feelings with him — or anyone for that matter? I was still at the point in my journey where I viewed myself, that child within me, as the enemy. I was the antagonist. I was to blame for everything. What if the people I loved found out the truth and rejected me? It was too risky to disclose my abuses. How could they ever understand? *I* didn't even understand it because I had not yet integrated the fractured parts of me. At the age of forty-one, I was *still* viewing my past through the eyes of that broken, uninformed, ignorant, and immature adolescent. This was the only view I had because the memory of the events had been so overwhelming for me at that age that my brain went into panic mode and imprinted them. And unbeknownst to me, these now imprinted memories and the terrifying emotions associated would become my daily companions.

It was easier to pretend I was okay.

But when the pretending became too overwhelming, I discovered alcohol.

# CHAPTER
# *SIX*

## ADDICTION

E ven though I came from a long line of alcoholics, including my father, alcohol was never a problem for me. Until my forties, I was always a social drinker. But unbeknownst to me, the genetic disease of alcoholism was passed down to me and was about to become completely unleashed with a vengeance. As the Big Book of Alcoholics Anonymous says, the disease of alcoholism is cunning, baffling, and powerful. And the Big Book is right.

I learned this firsthand. Initially alcohol was my friend. It supported me in not analysing or thinking about my suffering or my traumas. I never discussed my past or my myriad of emotions (which I now know were Emotional Flashbacks) with anyone, including my husband. I kept it all a secret — a deep, dark secret. However, I have learned that it is completely impossible to numb only one emotion. When someone tries to numb only her sadness, at the same time she inevitably also numbs her ability to feel joy or excitement.

To the world, I appeared to have it all and be successful. But inside, I was slowly dying from feelings of unworthiness, anxiety, and constant confusion.

It was when my father was dying that I began to drink more regularly and I justified it by saying I deserved it; I was grieving my dying father. But secretly, I loved the effect alcohol had on me. I was finally calm. My brain stopped spinning. I could breathe again. There was a ceasefire in my brain. That raging internal war was temporarily put on hold. Alcohol helped numb my feelings every evening. But sadly, the battle and the feelings resumed the second I opened my eyes the next morning. This vicious cycle continued day after day.

Unfortunately, one drink was not enough, and my drinking started to escalate. I became scared, thinking I was going to end up like my father — an angry alcoholic, something I'd always despised about him. As a result, I did what was familiar to me, I pushed away that thought. But then I began to self-medicate by drinking more. I told myself I couldn't possibly be an alcoholic. I wasn't living on a park bench drinking out of a brown paper bag. I was a well-respected mother and wife. I had a job.

But alcohol does not discriminate. It doesn't care if you are homeless, a housewife, or a professional. It doesn't care about your race, gender, or religion.

Unknown to many people, alcoholism is a *disease*. For those who have this disease, once alcohol enters our bodies, a chemical reaction takes place in our brains that makes us completely unable to stop drinking. This is why we embarrass ourselves, pass out, and even black out. Alcoholics are warned over and over that it is *the first drink* that is the problem, not the second or fifth. We must stay away from that *first* drink to prevent the chemical reaction from taking place. And when addicts aren't drinking or drugging, they are thinking and obsessing about using. It is a disease that centers in the mind.

If a person has the genetic predisposition to this disease and the circumstances are right, she may find herself completely and utterly at its mercy. She may find, as I did, that she is powerless over alcohol. A person will completely loose her ability to choose whether or not to drink. Alcohol will own every single part of her — her mind, body and, most significantly, her spirit.

Before long I began blacking out from drinking. I was isolating. Falling down. Pushing my beautiful children and husband away. Wanting to be left alone. I loathed everything about myself. And soon, the only feeling I chased was numbness. Obliteration. I wanted to disappear. Not feel.

That little girl inside me was now screaming for me to save her from the hell in which she existed. But I couldn't. I was terrified and I didn't know how to find her. I didn't even know if I wanted to find her. I intuitively knew there was something I was not supposed to think about, something I didn't want to remember, but these memories were patiently waiting to be unearthed and exposed. My God, what was underneath all the repression? The façade? The alcohol?

It was her, my inner child, and she was so very broken.

After a year of this self-destructive behaviour, my father finally passed away. I have no regrets. My own alcoholism has been a gift in that it gave me an understanding as to the pain he must have been in for his entire life. Unlike me, he never found a twelve-step program to help him with his demons. He never reached out for help and so he carried whatever his burden was all alone. How sad that a human being should carry such pain all alone. But he did mellow and soften as he got older. His multiple illnesses made drinking impossible for him and this gave me a few years of an authentic relationship with him. I am also thankful I was with him as his soul made the transition into his next journey. When I am asked to speak at an A.A. meeting, I sometimes refer to The Butterfly Story.

Immediately after my father passed away, I turned on my phone to text a friend. My profile picture, which had been a picture of my dad, had been mysteriously changed to a picture of a butterfly. I later found out that it was my then seven-year-old daughter who did this.

She had somehow managed to figure out my passcode, get into my phone, and then go into its settings and choose a butterfly as my new picture. I was stunned because she was never allowed to play with my phone and was completely unfamiliar with how it worked. Of all the pictures she could have chosen, it was a butterfly. Coincidence? The Universe? Whatever the reason, butterflies symbolize transformation. At that moment I was positive it was a sign that my dad had been transformed, that he was no longer in pain and was with his Creator.

Today, I don't think that was it at all. Now I think it was a sign for ME. My inner child, in the guise of my daughter, gifted me with a butterfly mere minutes after one of my abusers, my father, died. Perhaps this symbolic child was saying, *He is gone now. You can stop this madness of trying so hard to fix him and feel his love. It is time for you to stop drinking and begin the process of emerging and breaking free from this chrysalis, that dark and lonely cocoon you have trapped and isolated yourself in. Break free from the bondage of alcoholism and suffering. Then, and only then, will you find me. And in finding me, you will find yourself. You will find who you truly are, and the most glorious transformation will take place.*

For another year, though, I stayed in the safety and protection of that cocoon. I was a shell, completely empty and void of everything. I was on autopilot. I pretended to be this amazing person during the day at work, come home utterly exhausted from my performance, make dinner, and then drink. I would take pills, wash them down with rye, and pass out on the couch.

Sleep.

Wake up.

Repeat.

I had to carry on this charade because I was sure if people knew the real me, including my husband, they would despise and abandon me. I am also ashamed to admit that I thought nothing of the consequences that my drinking had on my husband or children. It got to the point where I didn't care about anything. I was completely apathetic. I couldn't fathom the idea that I was fucking up other people's lives along with my own. I only thought of numbing the pain. That is until the day the universe intervened and literally saved my life.

By that time, I was not actively suicidal, but I did not want to exist on this planet anymore. I realized I was either going to die from drinking or I was going to have to figure a way to live without it. I needed to make a choice.

There is a journal entry somewhere in my house that I wrote just before my father died. Or maybe it was after. I wrote it drunk while sitting on his empty bed. It felt like it was the beginning of the end of my life. I was stuck in the horrors of C-PTSD without knowing it. I could NOT, no matter how hard I tried, stop drinking. This journal entry was written on one of my darkest days. I wrote about the black hole that was swallowing me up. I was so lost, hopeless, bewildered, and confused. I wrote:

> *What the fuck has happened to my life?*
>
> *I have everything a girl could want yet I have nothing.*
>
> *I am a wife, **but I am a drunk.***
>
> *I am a mother but I am a drunk.*
>
> *I want to be a good mother, a loving mother, but yet, I am a drunk.*
>
> *How did this happen?*
>
> *I love my husband and children with everything I am. I want so badly to give them my whole heart, but I don't know how to do this because my heart is shattered into a million pieces.*
>
> *Which piece should I give them?*
>
> *The one that holds the shame of a thousand sinners?*
>
> *The one that aches with such profound sadness?*

*The piece that contains the rage that I don't even understand.*

*Or maybe I should give them the crazy piece because this is the part I know best; the confusion that drives me and makes me question myself over and over and over.*

*No.*

*It is better that I stay drunk. They are safer that way.*

*They won't want any part of my heart.*

I had crossed that invisible line from social drinking into full blown alcoholism and I knew I was powerless over it. My bottom came, symbolically, in the form of a little girl.

I was awakened in the middle of the night by my daughter. As usual, I had passed out on the couch the previous evening. She gently shook me and asked me if I was okay. I was confused, so I asked her why she was asking me this. She said, "Mommy, don't you remember? You fell down the stairs tonight."

I didn't remember. And I had broken my hand.

When I woke the next day, I was mortified and so ashamed that my seven-year-old was checking on ME — her mom — to make sure I was okay.

What was happening to my life? It was spinning out of control. And just when I thought it couldn't get any worse, it did. I realized that my seven-year-old daughter was starting to parent me.

Something had to be done. I couldn't stop drinking no matter how hard I tried and the thought of my children growing up with what I had grown up with was too unimaginable to bear.

Because of this, one night I took a handful of pills and drank a fifth of rye. I seriously did not care whether I woke or not. I truly felt there wasn't any hope anymore; I was always going to be a burden to everyone and they would be better off without me. I just could not exist in this mental torture anymore. I was convinced that I was beyond help.

When I did wake up the next morning, I intuitively knew the time had come. I told my husband I needed help to get over what I thought at the time was my only problem: drinking.

He took me to the hospital where I was placed in a locked room and was eventually seen by a psychiatrist. I remember this doctor focusing solely on my drinking. I don't recall him asking me anything about my pain or my emotional state, let alone considering that what I had done the previous evening could be seen as attempted suicide.

I have learned that most people do not understand the disease of alcoholism, and that includes doctors. They think we are *choosing* to drink. We are not. We lost the power of choice a long time ago. The majority of alcoholics don't want to drink but it's a compulsion beyond human control. Drinking is not our problem, it's our *solution*. It is our solution to everything we experience in life. It stops us from feeling. And trust me, we loathe ourselves because we cannot stop drinking and hurting the people we love the most.

At the hospital, it was evident I was a nuisance, a drunk, and he suggested I go to detox. Not only was I humiliated, I was also devastated that I didn't receive the help I thought I would get. But the universe works in mysterious ways. A gift came out of this darkness. My pain was so intense, so profound, that I reached out to whatever God was out there.

It was a prayer from the depths of my soul and it was only three words. That night, as I lay in that hospital bed alone and frightened, I whispered, "Please help me." Whatever God or Creator was out there at that time, it heard my prayer and answered it.

I went home and started calling various treatment centers. One in particular stood out because the intake coordinator was so kind and understanding towards me. She spoke with me for over an hour and shared her own recovery journey. However, she said the wait list to get in was over three months long. I couldn't wait three months, let alone three weeks. I was terrified I would continue drinking.

And so I called her every single day to see if anyone had cancelled. She gently told me cancellations rarely happen. On day five she called me at work and said, "You are not going to believe this. This never happens. Someone just cancelled. If you can get all your paperwork done within two days, the spot is yours". Fortunately (or providentially) I already had a scheduled appointment with my family doctor the next day so he was able to do everything I needed. So on that Monday, on a cold and snowy February morning, I walked through the doors of this treatment center that had a huge butterfly on its door. And this very spiritual and healing treatment center completely changed my life.

I read somewhere recently that trauma "is the real gateway drug to addiction." I believe this to be completely true because studies show that trauma victims are more likely to suffer from addiction issues than the non-traumatized population. The pain and confusion from childhood trauma is incredibly severe, and if a person has no idea why they are experiencing this psychological suffering, escaping or numbing seems like a completely logical solution. Research also shows that other coping mechanisms for C-PTSD can include OCD, hypervigilance, dissociating, and even splitting into multiple personalities. Some, like me, drink and drug. Some become addicted to food or sex.

But there is no way you can even begin to heal from your trauma unless you deal with your addiction first. It just isn't possible. You have to be sober. You have to feel the pain, the fear, and all the other emotions you have numbed for so long.

I stayed at this treatment center for almost a month and "my obsession to drink" was lifted. I learned about the disease of alcoholism and about the twelve steps. It was there that I began my journey into *spirituality,* not religion. They are two completely different things. There is a saying in the rooms of A.A.- religion is for people who are afraid of going to hell, whereas spirituality is for those who have already been there. And I have been to hell multiple times.

I was completely convinced that because I had stopped drinking, everything else in my life would fall into place. I soon discovered, however, that without my solution of alcohol, the emotional pain became more acute. I was so terrified of picking up a drink again that I became very active in 12-step meetings and I did everything that was asked of me. The only thing I concentrated on during that first year was staying sober. I was away a lot and my husband took on the role of both mother and father. I still hadn't the faintest clue that I had C-PTSD. I thought I was just an alcoholic and the mental torture I was experiencing was alcoholism. I now realize the mental torture I was enduring was emotional flashbacks. The emotional flashbacks and the terror I was feeling in the present moment was me *re-experiencing, re-remembering, and re-feeling* the trauma of my past. But I didn't know this. I continued to believe I was just crazy. I would call my sponsor, crying, and ask her what I was doing wrong.

Little did I know that I was actually doing everything right; I was staying sober despite the pain. I was not reaching for a drink. It would be this gift of sobriety that would allow me to begin the arduous journey of dealing with my past. This happened in my second year of being sober.

# CHAPTER
# *SEVEN*

# WHEN THE STUDENT IS READY THE TEACHER APPEARS

I don't know if you believe in some kind of divine force guiding this universe, but in some way I always have. Initially, because I was raised Catholic, it was a religious god, but this is not the case anymore. Even in my darkest moments, when I doubted and felt abandoned by that angry religious god, a part of my being *knew* there had to be *something* out there, something far superior, benevolent, and more compassionate than what I had been taught God was.

I truly believe that it was not an accident that I met my trauma psychiatrist whom I shall call Dr. A. going forward.

It was the Divine, the goodness and benevolence of the Universe, that put him in my path. I had absolutely nothing to do with it and yet this man would become one of my greatest teachers and help heal my soul of all the pain and misunderstanding it had been carrying. He became the person who would show me how to chip away at the toxic shame I was immersed in, and make peace with that little girl inside me, a girl whom I'd wanted nothing to do with.

I was initially sent to this psychiatrist by my family doctor for a second opinion on my anxiety diagnosis. I specifically remember telling my family doctor that I would not go to see him; I just wanted to try a different medication. I was finished with doctors and therapists and their versions of what was wrong with me. He finally convinced me to go and see this particular psychiatrist, if only for this "quick" second opinion and then return to him to discuss what he had said.

To date, this quick second opinion has lasted eight years.

Dr. A. is not your typical psychiatrist. He utilizes various modalities, especially talk therapy, and is an expert in the field of childhood trauma and its treatment.

What are the chances that this would be the type of psychiatrist I was miraculously sent to?

When I first saw him, the subject of medication or previous diagnoses never came up. He simply asked me questions; questions that no one had ever asked me. And because I was so desperate for answers to the internal war, which was still raging, and so tired of lying, he became the first person I became completely vulnerable with. He was the first person I honestly told all my "secrets" to. Secrets I thought (at the time) should not matter anymore because my past was long gone. It was over. Done.

Many survivors I have worked with have said the same thing. They often say,

"I am older now, that was a long time ago, it doesn't/shouldn't matter."

If there is one point to be made, it is that it *does* matter. It doesn't matter if you are fifteen or fifty years old when you start processing your trauma. The brain and the body do not forget such life altering events. Trauma gets encoded into our very cells and changes the structure of our brains, especially in our amygdala, also known as our emotional response/fear center. (This is where our emotional memories are stored.)

Thankfully, by the time I saw Dr. A., I was sober, so emotionally broken and was done with all the pretending. I just didn't care. I told him in detail about the abuses the emotional state I eternally existed in, and the self-hatred I had towards myself. I remember not feeling anything when telling my story. I was so detached from it. Completely disconnected. Numb. It was as if I was recounting someone else's story, yet strangely it belonged to me. This too, is a very common behaviour by trauma survivors. There is often a lack of emotion when speaking of their abuse. This disconnection is actually a survival mechanism. It is the brain's way of shielding a survivor from the excruciating feelings brought on by abuse. By the end of that very first session, he looked at me and said, "You don't have OCD, you have Complex-PTSD."

Instantly, something in me shifted. I intuitively knew at my very core that he was telling the truth. I was *not* crazy. What I was experiencing were *symptoms*; symptoms of C-PTSD, symptoms of a completely *normal* reaction to a very abnormal childhood. And the symptoms associated with PTSD, if not understood correctly, can actually cause a person to feel crazy, as if she is losing her mind. Dr. A. then told me it was treatable and that we could meet on a regular basis if I was willing to do the work.

Dr. A. was the first person to give me hope. He told me he had worked with many patients whom he had seen through the exact same process and that they had healed; I only needed to trust in *my* ability to heal too. This sounded absurd. How could I heal from all the insanity in my mind? From the flashbacks? From never fully living in the present because my past was always in front of me, ruining everything? How could I possibly ever feel shame free? How was I supposed to let go of *decades* of old maladaptive coping mechanisms that were hard wired into my brain? He told me *all* of this was possible. But he said that it would take time and it would take work. And the work has proven to be gruelling, gut wrenching, enlightening, terrifying, and beautiful all at the same time. It has been so worth it.

I am learning that healing from trauma is not linear. A person doesn't just keep getting better and better as the months and years go by. There is no final destination. I have accepted that for the rest of my days on this earth I will be healing in some way, in some form. Sometimes it's emotional healing. Other times it is spiritual or physical. And pain always accompanies healing. To me, the process is more like climbing a treacherous mountain towards a summit. Some days you take a detour and haven't a clue where you are. You learn something new. You release old trapped energy. There are days when you take a giant step forward and are completely elated, only to be triggered by something that pulls you two steps backwards and you slide down a little.

This is normal. I used to get completely despondent and break down when this happened until I started to learn *and accept* that these periods are actually necessary and part of the healing journey. I fall. I stumble. I feel defeated. I get sad and angry. I grieve. I want to quit. I become terrified that I will slide down the trauma vortex. But I eventually get up and recover the ground I mistakenly thought I lost, and I continue the climb.

Dr. A. has compassionately and empathetically held my hand as I have had to walk through the battleground of my childhood and adolescence. He has allowed me to have a safe place where I can sob, rage, and question anything and everything from my past. He has helped me to see that I was the *victim* in all of this. I didn't cause any of my suffering, my abusers did.

This doctor constantly reminded me that I *already knew* the answers to all my pain. At first this used to really irritate me because I wanted him to just tell me how to get better, to just tell me what I needed to know so I could then just do it and move on from the suffering. He never did. There were multiple sessions where I left his office totally angry with him.

I now understand that he was helping me learn to trust and believe in myself, to look inside myself and find the answer, *my own answer and truth*.

No one on the planet can tell us what our truth is. Recovery from childhood abuse is a journey of rediscovering the self, the soul and we need to do this on our own. I can't tell anyone how they can recover, only that it is possible.

My answer, my truth, was found in that broken little girl I had avoided for decades.

To me, this is the Divine at work.

I have been successful in finally starting to re-write the story of my life. I am finally believing that I am *not* crazy, nor was I ever. I have stopped self-blaming myself for everything and anything that happened during my formative years. *I* did not cause my trauma, *I* did not cause my abuses and, therefore, *I* did not cause my PTSD. I was a child and therefore, totally blameless.

Trauma occurs when an event, or in my case many events, happen in a way that the mind finds totally incomprehensible. The logical part of our brain actually shuts down and the survival part of the brain kicks in. We then go into either fight, flight, freeze, or "fawn" mode, a term coined by survivor and therapist Pete Walker. We have no control which response will kick in. The brain cannot normally process these abnormal events and, therefore, the memories and the associated horrific feelings remain "stuck" in the limbic/mammalian part of our brains. If left untreated or unprocessed, PTSD can develop. The brain will then remind the person, sometimes through flashbacks, of the traumatic event in order to prevent it from happening again. Anything that reminds a person of the trauma can trigger a flashback. It could be a smell. A sound. A touch. C-PTSD is a memory disorder. When a person experiences a flashback, whether it is visual, emotional, body- or thought-based, it feels as if it is actually happening in the present, but in reality *it is only a memory* of the past traumatic event. It is the most confusing and terrifying feeling because it feels so real.

The brain *needs*, and is programmed, to remember the trauma in order to avoid it, but at the same time, the person is desperately trying to forget it.

Yes, you read that correctly.

The way I view this is that our brains are actually trying to protect us, to do us a favour. But the rational part of our mind is desperately trying to forget the suffering we endured. Therein lies the cause of the internal war that is waged endlessly within our souls.

Sadly, when trauma occurs in childhood and adolescence, the brain is still developing. The child lacks any kind of understanding as to why her caretakers are raging, abusing, or abandoning her. The child will unknowingly take on, absorb, and internalize her parents' shame, anger, and sadness and truly believe it's her fault. And with no other adult to tell her otherwise, the disorder takes root, and the shame cycle starts to spiral. This is happening just as all the millions of neural pathways in her brain are being formed. The circuits are developing. The messages are being cemented.

*You are worthless.*

*You are a failure.*

*You are crazy.*

Without any intervention, the child is doomed to believe these lies, these deceptions, and unknowingly may continue to participate in the maladaptive coping mechanisms and the charade in which she lives.

I, for example, had always assumed and been told that I had Obsessive Compulsive Disorder. This was because of the intrusive thoughts I constantly endured for decades. It wasn't until I started trauma therapy that I realized every single one of my thought obsessions *all* had their roots in my primary and secondary trauma. These intrusive thoughts were once upon a time actually *helping* me deal with my trauma. They were my friends, amazing strategies that my inner child used to survive everything she was trying to cope with. Once I understood this and began processing the root causes of my intrusive thoughts, I was able to slowly begin the process of letting go of this torturous coping mechanism. Today, if I experience an old intrusive thought, I metaphorically hold that broken little girl and remind her that her thoughts are perfectly normal for what she endured, but are now are no longer necessary. She is safe. She has me.

I wrote earlier that it felt as if my brain felt a war was going on. What I didn't know then, is that there actually *was* a war going on — a war between my adult self and my younger self. My trauma(s) caused my psyche to become fractured. It shattered and then repressed the parts of me that I hated and was ashamed of. Dr. A. told me that until I integrated and accepted those parts, I would never be whole. I would never be free. Those broken parts were screaming at me to acknowledge, validate, understand, and forgive. But I didn't think it was possible. How could I find, let alone forgive and connect with, that little girl inside me? I wanted *nothing* to do with her.

I hated her.

As far as I was concerned, she had totally fucked up my life. My toxic shame had convinced me that she was to blame for everything that had made my life go so horribly wrong. The idea I could even befriend this inner child seemed ludicrous. But I had to try. What choice did I have? I could kill myself. I could start drinking again to numb the pain, a slower form of suicide. But was this the legacy I wanted to leave for my own children — that they had an alcoholic mother who committed suicide?

Was I going to destroy their lives as well mine?

I also had to try to recover for my husband who had, until then, walked through every flashback and symptom I experienced with such compassion and patience. I recall nights where I would be unable to sleep and would be sitting alone on the couch terrified and sobbing. He would come downstairs and just sit with me; he wouldn't say anything but his quiet presence was so comforting. Once, during a couples therapy session my husband was asked point blank why he was still with me after all the drinking and isolating I did. I will forever remember his answer. He said, "Because I know underneath all that pain is still the girl I fell in love with."

I carry this message with me in my heart every single day.

The first step in healing from my childhood trauma was going back to my childhood memories and talking about them in detail. This was done in a safe environment over very long sessions.

I told Dr. A. I felt unworthy and a burden to everyone. I had convinced myself since childhood that I was the bad one, not my abusers. In fact, I don't even recall being angry at what they had done. It all seemed so normal. I must have done something to deserve it, I must have done something to be treated that way. The only emotion I knew at that time was shame. Toxic, soul-crushing shame.

Shame. That word alone causes such profound sadness because it is the one primary emotion that has driven me my entire life. No human being should ever have to exist in this darkness. Shame and guilt are two different things.

Guilt can be positive, it says "I did something bad" and offers a person the opportunity to learn from the mistake and move on.

Shame on the other hand, says "I *am* bad."

As Brene Brown wrote, "Shame is the intensely painful feeling that we are unworthy of love and belonging."

She also states that "The antidote to shame is empathy and connection and we need to be vulnerable and share our stories. And once we own our painful stories, we can then rewrite the ending." I love this. I am determined to write a beautiful ending to my story.

I lived with toxic shame for almost my entire existence without ever fully understanding its root cause, its irrationality, and hence my internal struggles.

Now that I know the truth and understand the real story of my childhood, I will no longer, for *her,* my inner child's sake, allow this toxic shame rule me. It is no longer welcome in my soul because I never did anything wrong. My only sin was believing that I had. Even this belief was something I absorbed from my abusers.

Until recently, I used to think that if only I had been stronger as an adolescent, if only I had told someone, if only I hadn't done this or that, maybe things could have been different.

But this is futile because I cannot change my past and I cannot change the fact that I became immersed in toxic shame and developed C-PTSD. What I *can* do is *view* my past differently now, from the correct perspective, the real story. I am not to blame. I was a child, a teenager. The blame lies squarely on those adults who were supposed to care, love, protect, and nurture me. Their job was to help me blossom into the person I was meant to be. And they utterly and completely failed in that area.

After a few years of one-on-one therapy, I still felt there was a piece missing from my healing. I had learned so much from Dr. A., and I completely understood what had happened to me and why I reacted the way I did. But I longed to be with others like me who understood these issues and the symptoms that surround childhood trauma. I needed what I now know is *connection* with others like me.

This led me to a non-profit organization in Toronto called The Gatehouse. The Gatehouse is a safe place for adult survivors of childhood sexual abuse. It is run mainly by peer facilitators who have been affected by sexual abuse. They have various group programs for both men and women.

I initially participated in their Phase One women's program, which lasted for fifteen weeks. It was very empowering. I had finally found a place where there were other survivors just like me who had been through very similar experiences. The facilitators stated at the beginning of the session that there was no such thing as "trauma trumping." Trauma was trauma. Whether you had been sexually abused once, twice, or a hundred times, I learned that it doesn't matter. Whether it was a brutal rape or molestation, the results and the damages that transpire from these experiences are the same. For a girl like me, who completely minimized my sexual abuse my entire life, The Gatehouse was the first place I felt I could truly belong and be comfortable. We all spoke the same language. I could be vulnerable, completely raw, and talk openly about something that had happened or something I had done that I was ashamed of. Many of the survivors would nod, smile, and say, "me too." The relief I felt was indescribable. It was powerful. We became a tribe and worked through many issues together. I was no longer alone.

My experience at The Gatehouse was so overwhelming that I decided to train to become a peer facilitator myself. Today, I help facilitate a women's only group and it is so very humbling to be part of their journey. I have witnessed first-hand the profound healing that happens when people find the courage to be vulnerable and share their stories, their shame, and their secrets.

Tragically, I've also witnessed the devastation childhood abuse continues to have on adult men and women. Some survivors continue to be consumed by their trauma and shame and cannot do the inner child exercises. They speak of how they still and might always despise that part of themselves. I once felt that way too. Some could not finish the group and left before the sessions were over. But this beautiful place The Gatehouse never closes for anyone. It accepts wherever a person is on his or her healing journey. It invites them to come back whenever they are ready and in the meantime, offers them other supports, such as one-on-one counselling or referrals to other organizations. It is truly remarkable and is one of the few places in all of Canada that offers this type of program to adult survivors of childhood abuse. And sadly, it is in desperate need of funding.

My hope is that someday all survivors of sexual abuse will find the courage to connect with that broken part of themselves. Only then will they realize they did not cause their brokenness. Only then will they realize recovery is possible. They too will find, as I did, that it is their inner child who holds the key to the healing they so desperately need. Not every survivor is lucky enough to have access to an actual psychiatrist who specializes in childhood abuses and who cares as deeply for his patients as Dr. A. does. So places like The Gatehouse are absolutely essential to people who lack the money or access to private therapy, and aid them in not feeling alone on this journey of rebuilding their souls. Individual and group therapy were crucial in the process of rebuilding of my life. It turns out I needed a tribe, a village to help me heal.

I will *not* give one more day of my life back to my abusers. They have already stolen too much from me. If I have days where my brain goes back to those old beliefs, which it still does, I now know what to do. I no longer panic. Instead, I reach out for her — that freckled-faced kid inside me. And we sit together on the wooden stairs in my childhood home and I allow her to cry in my arms for as long as she needs me. I remind her of the truth — that she is so beautiful and courageous and together we shatter the lies.

What you will read is known as my truth. They are, and continue to be, the healing dialogues I have written to my inner child when I was recovering from the torment of my traumas.

It is my greatest hope that this healing happens to you too. I pray that you will find your own truth. No one else can find it for you. I urge those who are reading this not to quit. Be brave. Be courageous. You may not know it yet, but you too have a warrior within you. She has already survived the actual war. If you don't know where to start, pick up a pen. Breathe. Quiet your mind. Introduce yourself to her. Ask her what she needs from you. The answers will eventually come. She has been waiting a long time.

# CHAPTER
# *EIGHT*

## EARLY YEARS

I was born in the winter of 1968. Through conversations with my mother, I have come to understand that I must have been somewhat "abandoned" since birth. I wasn't dropped off on the steps of a fire station or placed in an orphanage and put up for adoption. That is not the kind of abandonment I mean. I'm referring to emotional abandonment.

Over the years, my mother has said many times that she often left me crying in the crib as a baby because she "didn't have time to tend to my needs with my two older sisters running around." As I process this, I understand how overwhelmed she was, but still, I was just a baby. An infant. Totally helpless. It is a documented fact that babies *need* human touch and comfort to thrive. To feel safe. To feel loved. I had those same needs and those needs were not met. I do believe that my deep sense of unworthiness and abandonment quite possibly began at the beginning of my life.

Because of my mother's behavior toward me as an infant, and before I could even utter a word, the notion that I was not important was seeping into my soul. I was alone. There was no one in my world to comfort me when I needed it.

I grew up in a home that outsiders would call normal. More important, even I thought my upbringing was normal. It was all I knew. I had nothing to compare it to. But now, as an adult, I realize it was anything but normal. Behind the red brick exterior of our house, beyond the perfectly manicured lawn and gorgeous backyard garden, I lived with my mother, father, and two older sisters. When I look back now, I can see that we were always fractured. We never functioned as cohesive unit. We rarely spent time with each other and there was no real interaction in any meaningful sense. My sisters, however, did spend time with each other, but they never let me tag along. And I didn't have many friends so I was alone a lot. I believe this is when I developed my first coping mechanism which helped ease the loneliness I felt every single day. I fantasized constantly about having a different family. I created these wonderful stories in my head where I had an amazing family and lots of friends. In these fantasies, I was loved and liked by all who knew me. I was special. I was wanted. I was happy.

The only memory I have of our family being together was at dinnertime. We ate dinner promptly at six, but afterwards, everyone went their separate ways.

I never once witnessed any love or affection between my parents. My dad worked in an office from nine to five. My mother worked evenings and weekends as a part-time nurse. Both my parents were emotionally unavailable. My mom was not nurturing towards any of us. This was probably because she had not been shown how to nurture others. She'd lost her mother at an early age and was brought up in a convent. She is still alive.

My dad also lost a parent at a young age. It has only been lately that I have realized that he never spoke of his past or of his birth family. And strangely, I never asked about them. I know absolutely nothing of my paternal grandparents, the people who helped shaped my father. I wish I had asked about them. He was a quiet man and seemed to prefer his own company. He also seemed to prefer alcohol over his family. My parents did provide the basics, the necessities... food, clothes, shelter, the odd vacation, but that was all. But what value do these basics have when a child just wants and needs to feel loved and worthy?

My father would come home from work, change his clothes, and soon I would hear the clink of ice in the glass, the gin being poured, the lime being sliced. The energy in the house would begin to shift. He would retreat to the living room to escape behind the newspaper. Or if it was summer, he would go straight to his garden and tend to *its* needs, not ours. I remember constantly trying to gauge his mood. Was it safe to talk to him? Did he seem upset and in need of help? And if I sensed that he needed help, I would do anything to try to fix it.

Somehow, even as a child, I must have sensed a sadness in him because even when I was very young I always tried to engage with him, talk to him, entertain him. That was my role. The fixer. I wanted my dad to be happy and it made me sad when seemed upset. And sometimes, he would become violent when he was upset. It terrified me.

*Oh, my sweet girl, you are safe now.*

*I need you to know that trying to fix him was NOT your role. It NEVER was your role. You could not possibly have known what demons he was dealing with. You did not have any power to change him. But bless you for trying.*

*You should have been outside having fun and just being a kid. And HE should have encouraged you to do this... In fact, he should have participated in the occasional childhood play with you!*

*Even though you kept trying to be noticed, I know you always felt invisible. You must have felt so lonely. I am so sorry baby girl.*

> *Shame on HIM for not seeing you.*
> *Shame on HIM for choosing alcohol over you.*
> *You were so precious and innocent and had a heart*
> *of gold. I know you didn't like his sadness. So, in your*
> *childhood ignorance, you took on HIS sadness. But*
> *this was never yours to take, it never belonged to you.*
> *I need you to give all the sadness you feel in your soul,*
> *back to him. It is HIS sadness you feel, not yours.*
> *Give it back to him.*

My mother worked evening shifts and weekends, so they were rarely together. And when she was home, he would stay in the living room and she would go downstairs to watch television. I know my mom wanted a connection with him because during my teenage years, I would catch her crying about her loneliness. I tried to fix that too. I was terrified that they would get divorced. It was better for me to have two unhappy parents than for our already fractured family to split up. I used to tell my dad to take her out; I would even offer and give suggestions...take her out for dinner. Go to the movies. Show her love. I remember once confronting him angrily about why he drank. He told me that it was because he did not love my mother.

I was stunned.

Gutted.

Devastated.

What parent tells their child that? What parent allows their CHILD to suggest ways to fix THEIR broken relationship? I now see how fucked up that was.

This is the insanity that I can now see I lived with. I know, after being in recovery for alcohol abuse for almost eight years, that my father was doing what we alcoholics all do. He was isolating. Obliterating some kind of pain inside him. And because he died never talking to anyone about what that was, I will never know what pain he carried. Pain he carried all alone, not allowing anyone to help him.

*But you see my beauty, it was the disease of alcoholism that caused him to isolate from everyone, including you.*

*You had no power to compete with this disease. And, my God, you tried to fix that too. I know you did. You asked him to stop. You asked him why he drank so much. It must have been so painful to hear your dad tell you that he did not love your mother.*

*Jesus, how brutal that must have been. You craved, as all children do, his attention, his approval, his love. Anything. But sadly, that sense of rejection also seeped into your soul.*

*But you need to know there was nothing about you to be rejected; you were beautiful and perfect and full of light.*

*Let go of his rejection. His rejection was NEVER about you.*

*He drank to reject some part of himself.*

My father was a good man and that is why it is so hard to write about him, especially because he mellowed and became softer as he got older. He stopped drinking. He became more emotionally available. But sadly, the damage from my childhood remained. I was not yet in recovery when he was diagnosed with terminal cancer and I was therefore still in complete denial about my upbringing. Shockingly, we had only a few days with him before he passed and I told him what a good father he had been. I remember him looking at me with tears in his eyes and murmuring something to the effect that he hadn't been. How sad to have such regrets at the end of this earthly life. Today I view this as his amends to me. His eyes were his voice.

It was me who held his hand and loved him as he passed into the next life. I am forever grateful that I was there. It truly marked a transition for both of us.

In the beginning of my trauma therapy, I could not utter a bad word about him because it felt as if I was somehow betraying him.

My brain still felt that it had to protect *him*, as if the physical violence I endured at his hands as a child and teenager was acceptable. It was as if I needed to believe that all the things he'd done to me were somehow okay simply because he was my dad. I couldn't let anyone know he wasn't perfect. I couldn't allow *myself* to know he wasn't perfect. I remember one therapy session in particular where we focused solely on my father's behaviour towards me. I was completely honest about it. As I was driving home I started panicking at the thought of what I had said and had to pull the car over to catch my breath. I started sobbing. That little girl in me had spoken the truth about her daddy and she was terrified of the consequences.

Since I have become a parent, my perspective has changed. His treatment of my sisters and me was totally unacceptable. I was not constantly physically abused but he could fly into an absolute rage in the blink of an eye and become violent. This usually happened after he had been drinking. We would be sitting at the dinner table, someone would say something, and suddenly he was banging his fists on the table and plates were bouncing and clattering. During these times, I would instinctively bolt from the table if I knew his anger was directed at me. I would run and try to hide. Usually he chased me. There is no use in recounting all of the violent incidents, but I will write about two that stand out in my mind, if only to illustrate how abuse affects and confuses a child.

One evening, when my parents had guests over for dinner all the children were running around and laughing in the house. Out of the blue, my dad excused himself from his guests and calmly asked to see *me* in my room. As I entered my room, he grabbed me, threw me on the bed, and started choking me with both hands. I remember thinking that I couldn't breathe and might die. I can still see the absolute rage in his eyes. I actually remember being so confused and thinking *Why is he doing this? Why me? What did I do that my sisters weren't doing? Maybe I shouldn't have been having fun. Maybe I shouldn't have been laughing.*

He finally let go of my neck and I fell to the floor. As I lay there, he kicked me. And oddly, all of this happened in complete and utter silence because the guests and my mother were close by. I must have known this because I didn't cry, protest, or scream for help. I was silent. I don't remember much more except crawling into my closet and staying there. I wanted to be away from his hatred. I wanted to be left alone. I hated everything and everyone, especially my sisters, because they had not been punished. It was only me. Me. And no one, not one person, came searching for me or came to the aid of that shattered little girl. And because of this, my self-blame and shame grew even stronger.

> *Oh my God. I want you to know I am with you right now in the closet, my love.*
>
> *My poor, poor, beautiful girl. Can you feel me? Can you feel my arms around you?*
>
> *You did NOT deserve to be treated this way.*
>
> *You did NOTHING wrong.*
>
> *He is a fucking bastard for doing that.*
>
> *But I am here now, lying right beside you. Can you feel me? I have my arms wrapped tightly around you and I am stroking your hair. It is not your fault baby girl. He was wrong. You did nothing wrong. EVER. HE. WAS. WRONG!! HIM!! Not you.*
>
> *Let me love you. Please let me love you.*
>
> *Open your heart and let me heal all that fear and confusion and hate that was put inside you by them.*
>
> *Let me show you how precious you are. You are so loved and so beautiful.*
>
> *It's HIS fault he can't see this. HIS FAULT. He had no right to take HIS issues out on you. You had every right to scream at him and at your mom and even at the guests. You can scream now. Scream as fucking loud as you need to. Scream that you hate him.*

> *Hit him. Rage, rage, and let out all the unfairness and*
> *hurt and injustice of all HIS abuse.*
> *YOU WERE A CHILD.*
> *It was HIS role to love, protect, and nurture you.*
> *He should have welcomed your joy, your happiness.*
> *He failed utterly and completely.*
> *Your parents don't deserve you.*
> *But I, the one who once abandoned you too, am*
> *here and I will never, ever let you go.*
> *You will have me for eternity.*

Another time, when my mother was working, I fell off my bicycle and skinned my knees. They were bleeding and I went home to get a Band-Aid (and most likely sympathy). I was very upset. I walked into the kitchen, crying. My dad, who was loading the dishwasher, turned around and started laughing at me. To this day I do not understand why anyone would laugh at a crying child. But he did. For some reason, his laughter caused me, a ten-year-old, to become completely unhinged. I screamed at him. I unleashed a wrath in me that I didn't know existed. And I paid for that wrath. His eyes spoke volumes and I knew I had made a very bad mistake by yelling at him. I ran from the kitchen and he chased me right up the stairs. He caught me and I must have fallen because he dragged me by my legs into my room. He was screaming at me and kicking me. I was so afraid that I peed myself. When he saw the pee, he accused me of bringing water into my room, something that wasn't allowed in our household, and started kicking me harder. Again, it was so confusing. Just a few minutes earlier I had come to him for comfort and here I was, lying on the ground, far more injured than just my skinned knees.

> *Oh my baby girl. My poor, poor baby girl.*
> *Come here.*
> *Show me your knees. Let me clean them up for*
> *you and kiss them all better. That must have been so*

*scary when you fell off your bike. Let me hold you in my arms and rock you. Let me wipe away your tears.*

*I totally understand why you yelled my sweet girl. In fact, I am proud that you yelled, he deserved that. He should never have laughed at you when you were crying. Never. That was SO WRONG of him. That is not what a father does. He should have washed your knees and put a bandage on them. He should never have kicked you because you yelled or made you feel it was wrong for expressing your emotions. He should have asked you why you were so upset instead of punishing you. Emotions are meant to be felt and expressed. Your parents should have taught you how to do that properly.*

*But I am here now and I will help you handle all these crazy emotions you feel. There is nothing, absolutely nothing, that you can feel or think that is going to make me love you any less. Nothing. It is completely safe now for you to open up your heart and your mind and feel all of those old feelings.*

*These feelings are just repressed energy and you need to let them go. Let them go my love. Stay in my arms and let them go.*

What do I say about my mother? I love her, but I pity her. I see a sadness in her too. But she too, albeit unknowingly, contributed to my feelings of unworthiness because she was never nurturing or affectionate. Her biggest betrayal, though, is that she did not protect me. I remember her shutting the doors and the windows when my dad was in one of his rages and had me up against a wall. To me, this implies that what the neighbours might hear and think was more important than the fact that her husband was abusing her daughter. Maybe she was scared of him.

I have heard people say, "Oh times were different then, parents disciplined differently." This means nothing to me. Nothing. It is total bullshit. I am a parent. I have a son and a daughter. When I think of what I would do if my husband ever did that to one of our children, my entire perspective changes. I would tear him off of them. Maybe I would call the police. I do know that I would go to any lengths to protect them. Her reactions to his rage made me feel that I couldn't talk to her or confide in her about the pain he was causing me. Who was I to go to for support as a child or a teenager? My drunk father? My absent mother? My sisters who ignored me? Shouldn't every child have someone, *anyone*, they can go to no matter what has happened? That I felt I had no one to talk to had devastating consequences.

> *Oh my sweet girl. It must make you so angry that your mom didn't protect you from your dad's rages. It must be so hard for you to feel like you can't go to your own mother when you need her the most.*
>
> *Every child needs a mother, especially a little girl.*
>
> *You must feel so abandoned that she doesn't come and hold you or talk to you, especially when Dad gets angry at you. You deserve to have the most caring mother in the world because you are so, so precious and beautiful.*
>
> *She was never shown how to nurture and perhaps this is why she was unable to nurture you.*
>
> *I am going to be your momma now.*
>
> *Let me take care of you.*
>
> *I am going to give you all of those things you wish you had in a mother.*
>
> *I am going to love you, cherish you, protect you, and never, ever abandon you. I will come to you whenever you need me. You can talk to me about anything whenever you want. I will never judge you. You are free to be exactly who you are supposed to be.*
>
> *Just let me love you.*

# CHAPTER
# *NINE*

## DEATH OF MY SOUL

I dread writing about this part of my childhood because it is the story that altered the course of my life.

I avoided and repressed these events for decades, and in doing so, caused the toxic shame that kept me in a mental prison for most of my life. I never thought I would *ever* get over this. I was convinced that I was bad to my very core, that what I had done was so terrible it would go with me to my grave. This secret would be mine, and mine alone for eternity.

But, with Dr. A.'s empathy and guidance, and the courage of the little girl who endured this abuse, I slowly began to have enough trust in him to begin to peel back and share the layers of this part of my life. In doing so, I eventually discovered how wrong my perception of the events had been. He told me that even though I was a forty-something-year-old woman talking with him, I was not viewing my sexual abuse through my adult eyes; my traumatic breakdown had encoded into my brain *my adolescent's view* of the events and, therefore, I did not know any other version.

Although this is extremely difficult to write about and revisit, I feel compelled to share this massive part of my history in the hope that it will save someone else from enduring the mental torture I put myself through. I never want another human being to take on the shame of another person's actions, as I did.

There will be no more silence and there will be no more secrets because from my adult perspective, I now understand that I did nothing wrong as a child and young teenager.

This is the part I **mistakenly** blamed my inner child for, the part that made me believe she was inherently and irrevocably bad and damaged beyond repair. This is the reason I put her in prison, without so much as a trial. Because I spoke of this to no one, I alone became the judge and the jury, and I convicted her. She was given a life sentence for a crime she did not commit.

My memories of my sexual abuse are
f r a g m e n t e d

In the memory, I am in my cousin's bedroom and my uncle is lying on the bed. It is summer and I am watching my family laughing outside through the bedroom window.

Technically, they are just a few meters away.

A train whistles in the distance.

Today, whenever I hear a similar whistle, I think of him and the abuse.

Why am even in the room?

Did he ask me to come?

How did I get here?

Was I looking for him?

He asks me to come over.

I get in the bed.

Why would a ten-year old do that?

Wait, am I ten? Maybe I am nine. Maybe I am eleven. I don't know. I think I am ten.

Have I done this with him before? I think I may have but I am not sure.

My god, it seems so normal, so natural to lie beside him.

He is kissing me and making me do something I don't want to do but I can't remember what it is and I start to feel afraid.

I don't know what it is I am afraid of.

Everything is blank now.

Blank.

Blank.

Blank.

What is this blankness?

I have wracked my brain trying to figure all of this out to the point of near madness. I don't remember anything else except him whispering, "Don't tell your father."

Did he say my father? Or did he say my parents?

I won't tell my father or anyone else for that matter. Even though I was scared, I felt special. The abuse felt almost ... normal. I finally feel noticed. I think I am proud of what happened.

I have since learned that this man was a serial abuser. Motherfucker.

And all my extended family still talk about what a great man he was and I stare at them numbly thinking..... if only you knew.

But he is dead. He's fucking dead and I never got the chance to confront him.

What I don't know yet is the devastation that this will cause for the rest of my existence.

What I don't know yet is that I will spend the next six years of my life, unknowingly and ignorantly seeking out this sexual feeling, a feeling that *he, a grown man,* introduced me to at the age of ten. I will innocently seek it out, sometimes in very inappropriate ways, and I will try to recreate this feeling wherever and however I can.

I don't know what the feeling is. I am too young. I just know it is special.

And it is this, **my young sexual reactivity to HIS abuse, my inappropriate sexual acting out,** that will forever taint my childhood, adolescence, and adulthood.

I will carry this misplaced guilt for the rest of my life. I will water it, nurture it, and tend to it daily until it blossoms into full-blown soul-crushing shame.

When the flashbacks and memories of this period in my life and my sexual reactivity resurface at the age of twenty, I will feel stunned. I will immediately think I am beyond help.

Those neural pathways of shame have been forming so effortlessly my entire life. They have been developing because of my parents' emotional neglect and my father's alcoholism and physical abuse. And now, with these horrifying sexual memories, seen and constructed through the eyes of an ignorant adolescent, my shame has now become toxic and cemented for what I believe will be a lifetime.

> *OH MY FUCKING GOD!!!*
> *What are you doing?*
> *Get the fuck away from her.*
> *GET OFF!!!!!*
> *YOU are a fucking monster. I FUCKING HATE YOU!!!!*

> *Baby girl, you don't even know what he is doing!!*
> *It's okay. It's okay. You're okay.*
> *Come to mama.*
> *It's not your fault. It's not your fault. It is NOT your fault.*
> *It is his fault. HIS. You haven't done anything wrong.*
> *Nothing. You're perfect. You're so unbelievably beautiful. You're just a*
> *baby, sweetheart.*

*I am here now, in the doorway. Look over here.*
*Can you see me?*
   *Get out of the bed and come over to me, honey.*
*Come into my arms.*
   *I will carry you out of this room forever.*
   *You will never, ever go back there.*
   *You will never have to see him again. Ever. I will*
*keep you safe and away from him forever. Mama is*
*going to stay with you forever.*

I have forever blamed myself for my childhood and adolescent sexual reactions to his abuse. It has taken me *years* to examine and re-examine again and again what happened to me and look at it in its accurate context; to look at it from an *adult's* perspective instead of with a traumatized adolescent's interpretation.

I was physically and sexually abused, neglected, and already immersed in shame because of this, and because of my skewed religious beliefs. I was in desperate need of love. I was sexually taken advantage of by a trusted uncle. How can anyone blame at ten-year-old girl for being molested by an uncle and, later on, reacting sexually in inappropriate ways because she liked the strange feeling and attention?

I now understand and accept that my reactions to this abuse were 100% NORMAL. Many sexually abused children react exactly as I did; they just don't know any better. They are too young, powerless, and ignorant.

A child's body will instinctively respond to the physical feelings associated with the abuse but it cannot yet connect to them in a "sexual" way. His or her still-developing brain cannot cognitively process what is actually happening. It is profoundly confusing. And because of this, it is very normal for children of sexual abuse to try to recreate that feeling. This Freudian term is known as Repetition Compulsion. Children will repeat their abuse in different ways to gain power and mastery over what their brain subconsciously knows was a totally helpless situation. This coping mechanism can last right into adulthood.

Because I did not disclose my abuse for decades (or my sexual reactions to it), when it came time to look at that little girl and that teenager, I was already so immersed in toxic shame that I wanted nothing to do with her. Hate is a word not strong enough to describe what I felt towards her. Time and time again in therapy I was told that until I forgave her and let go of the shame, I would be forever trapped in its bondage. To me, this seemed an impossible task.

What helped me immensely in this area was when my doctor challenged me to look at other ten-year-old girls, such as my daughter, and ask myself what I would do if she told me she was molested and had the same sexual reactions because of it? Would I blame her? Yell at her? Shame her? Condemn her the way I had condemned myself? I did just that, and I was stunned.

Once I (symbolically) replaced myself with another little girl, I began to see how self-abusive I had been towards myself. I asked myself, how I would respond if it had been my daughter? The answer was immediate and a no brainer.

I would embrace her, talk to her, and get her any professional help she required despite any obstacles. I would constantly reassure her that it was not her fault and she was beautiful, brave, and innocent. I would tell her that any sexual responses she had were normal and were nothing for *her* to be ashamed of. I would protect her and seek out her abuser to ensure justice was met.

Why then, was I not giving myself the same empathy? The same love?

It was at this point that the first inklings of self-compassion started to blossom within me. I could not believe how harshly I had judged myself and my inner child for something that was completely out of my control, power, and understanding. I finally asked for *her* forgiveness. Dr. A. had always alluded to the fact that my inner child was waiting to be forgiven but I could never figure out what she needed forgiveness from. Now I understood. She just wanted me to tell her that what she had done was okay. That she wasn't "bad." That I loved her despite all that had transpired. That she was beautiful. Perfect. Sane.

Eventually, I had so many emotions that needed to be released, and so many things I wanted my inner child to know, that I began journaling. And eventually, I started to write to the little girl inside of me. At first it was awkward and the entries were short. Initially, I just told her how sorry I was for blaming her and not acknowledging her all those years. This was all I could offer her at that time. But it was a start, and it was enough for us to begin the process of integration. The following is one of my earliest journals to her.

> *My beautiful girl.*
> *I do not know you yet, but I want to.*
> *I hope you want to know me.*
> *I am only beginning to understand all the things you endured and how alone you must have felt. I am so sorry I haven't acknowledged you. I know you have been so sad, and so terrified for years, and all I did was shut you down.*
> *You were abandoned by our family and then by me. Please know that it was the only way I knew how to survive. I didn't have any of the knowledge I now have, nor anyone to go to who could help me understand. I was so afraid too.*
> *Trust me, if I could go back and change the way I treated you, I would. I would sit with you and get you all the help you needed instead of running away from you. But I can't change the past.*
> *I hope you will let me try to get to know you. I think you are so brave.*

Writing to her became very therapeutic, insightful, and healing. The Gatehouse encouraged us to try to have our inner children write to us. During one session we sat quietly in a circle, listened to a guided meditation and, using our non-dominant hand, allowed our inner children to tell us what we felt they needed us to hear.

I felt that my little girl was asking me why I blamed and hated her. She told me she was very sad and lonely. It was extremely powerful. I told her it was because I hadn't known any better, and if I could, I would go back and change everything and not blame her.

My heart slowly began to feel her pain, the pain she had been carrying for decades. It was brutal and beautiful all at the same time. I was finally allowing those feelings, *her feelings*, to be expressed.

I promised her that I would try my best not to repress ANYTHING anymore, no matter how terrifying that idea was. I would not repress any thought, feeling, or memory. Whatever was to be revealed, would be revealed; we would always have each other.

Without a doubt, the courage to find my inner child, and then to forgive her for what my uninformed brain thought she was responsible for, turned out to be the beginning of the most beautiful love and trust that developed between us.

It was such a gift.

# CHAPTER
# *TEN*

# RELIGION VS SPIRITUALITY

G od.

That word stirs up a lot of emotions. There is a massive difference between religion and spirituality. Trust me, I have lived on both sides of those ideas.

I had a strict Catholic upbringing. I went to a Catholic school. I sang in the choir and was an altar server for most of my childhood. Church was a huge part of our family life and we never missed Mass.

I remember always longing for "God," whatever mysterious being that was, and mistakenly thinking I had one just because I attended service at a religious institution.

What I have come to realize, through therapy and especially through the Twelve Steps of Alcoholics Anonymous, is that the idea of God I had wasn't a "personal" God of *my own understanding*. It was a religious God, taught to me by someone else. That God was taught to me by my teachers, by my parents, and by the priests. I never once had the courage to question anything I was taught.

Tragically, what I absorbed and internalized from all these "teachers" was that God was cruel, vengeful, and condemning.

I am not criticizing the Catholic faith, nor any other faith for that matter. There were, and still are, things I love about my faith. I still attend mass sometimes and I love the sense of serenity. I love the music. I like the sense of community.

But for some reason, in my developing years, I was never taught about a forgiving, loving, and compassionate God, a benevolent God. I wished I had been taught that God was nothing but unconditional love; a beautiful celestial being who could offer comfort in times of hardship. My younger self could have really used *that* notion of God to comfort her. It actually may have changed the course of her life.

An abused child (or any child) does not need to believe there is an omnipotent presence who counts her sins and waits to punish her. She already lives with enough trauma, shame and self-hatred. That (mis)conception of God, among other things, was paramount to my experiencing my secondary trauma. My belief in a condemning, wrathful God, along with my adolescent misperception of my primary trauma, caused me to nearly lose my soul.

Literally.

It is the day I felt so worthless that I had to completely abandon my inner child and what I perceived that she had done in order to survive, to breathe, to not break into a billion pieces.

It is summer and it is warm in the house. The windows are open. I have just come home from my part-time job. I am sitting in my dad's green chair nonchalantly flipping through the Bible. I randomly come across a verse in the Old Testament that says something about perverse sexual acts and how anyone who engages in them is to be condemned to the fires of hell for eternity.

Suddenly, memories start to surface. I remember in vivid detail the sexual abuse from my uncle and what I thought were my abnormal (and now know through therapy were totally normal) sexual responses to it. I am horrified. I am petrified. In that moment, in that instant, my life is forever altered. NOTHING will ever be the same.

I am too young and I don't yet have all the facts. I don't have the knowledge and understanding of what has happened in my life up to this point. And because I don't yet possess this knowledge, *I traumatize myself.* And as a result, a secondary trauma occurs.

This trauma is far worse than what actually physically happened in my childhood.

I go to bed on this night a completely and totally changed person than the person I was when I woke that morning. In an instant I have convicted myself. Done. Over.

I. Am. Bad.

For years, a black dot has been festering in me from all the abuse, the neglect, abandonment, and misperception of God. Now this black dot has completely solidified. I believe with everything in me that I am the worst person on the planet.

And I truly believe I am going to hell.

I am absolutely terrified. Because of my already fractured relationship with my family, I have no one to tell, no one to talk to. Not a soul. I am so ashamed I can't even tell Anne. I am continuously crying and shaking and my mother keeps asking me what is wrong. I can't tell her. I need to fix this, she can't.

Somehow I get it in my head that I have the power to make this right with God. This is what is commonly known as magical thinking. Simply put, magical thinking is the belief that a person's ideas, thoughts, or actions can influence the course of events in the physical world. In my case, I believed if I tried hard enough, I could change the perception I thought God had of me.

I thought, I will become perfect. I will do everything God (the one I believed in at the time) wants me to do. I begin praying unceasingly, I make novenas, I go to confession repeatedly and plead for forgiveness for my childhood and adolescent sexualized behaviour. I do not mention my uncle. The priests brush it off and tell me not to worry about it. Even their absolution doesn't help. I ask this God to forgive me for being such an evil person.

I can't sleep. I lose weight. I am in constant fear.

But still, I tell no one.

My mom takes me to see a doctor to see if I can get medication that will calm me down. The doctor asks me what is wrong. I don't tell him what has happened. I don't get any medication.

I need to stuff down all the horrible memories that haunt me. I need them gone. The pretending begins.

I start to act as if everything is okay to my family and friends. I fucking hate myself and especially that little girl who did those things years ago. I push her down, down, down into the depths of the darkness inside where I won't ever have to see or think about her again. She is entombed for what I hope will be forever.

I don't know who I am anymore. I am SO traumatized I start to think I must be crazy and actually start looking for signs that I am crazy. My OCD fears kick in. What if I am crazy? What if I abuse a child? What if I am like my uncle? Oh my God, what if I totally lose control and do something horrendous? My brain is looking for evidence that I am none of those things and at the same time is terrified that I could be.

My brain and soul cannot comprehend what has happened. It embeds the memory. It encodes it. It will not let me forget it even though I am trying so hard to forget it.

My life is over even before it has begun.

And I am only nineteen years old.

I can see myself in the October twilight, months after I convicted myself. It is lightly raining outside and I am sitting on our wooden stairs, sobbing. No one is home. I am terrified that I am beginning to lose my mind. I am terrified that I haven't done enough to make things right with this God. I am terrified that this is going to be my life forever because I cannot erase what has happened. This terror becomes another trauma.

Am I forgiven? How will I ever know? I need proof that I am okay. I need proof that I have done enough to be in His good graces. I can't be happy until I have the proof that I have fixed all this chaos. Fixing, fixing, fixing is all I have ever known. Fix my dad. Fix my parents' marriage. Fix my family. And now, I need to fix me.

I absolutely despise that girl inside me. I am sure it's all her fault. She has totally and completely ruined my life. I feel as if I have no future. I think about killing myself. But that is a mortal sin and I would *definitely* go to Hell. So the only thing I can do is collect all the broken pieces of my soul, try to tape them together, then spend the rest of my days in atonement for what I think are **MY** sins.

> *Oh my God, my heart is breaking for you.*
> *It is breaking into a million different pieces because you have it so wrong. So, so wrong.*
> *You don't understand any of this, my love, because you've been so traumatized and you're still so young.*
> *You cannot even comprehend all the things that have happened already in your short life.*
> *LISTEN TO ME! YOU were the VICTIM in all this.*
> *I NEED you to know that NONE OF THIS WAS YOUR FAULT.*
> *Look at me. You were abused, sexually, physically, and emotionally. You were a fucking child.*
> *Come, I want you to lean into my arms and sob your eyes out. You are finally allowed to cry. I want you to cry and rage at the injustice of it all. I want you to fucking hurl all your fears, obsessions, and your need to fix yourself back at them. All of this suffering belongs to them. THEM.*
> *You are innocent. You did nothing wrong. THEY DID. You are NOT crazy, THEY are. You only feel*

*crazy because you are traumatized. TRAUMATIZED. That's all. Trauma makes a person feel like they are going crazy.*

*Your poor brain can't make sense of any of this, because NONE of this story makes sense.*

*Can I hold you? Please let me hold you.*

*I need to know that what you did was okay. You did nothing wrong. All of those sexual things you did as a kid and a young teen were okay. They were a completely normal response to what had happened to you. They were SO normal. You were just a kid with no one to talk to about it.*

*It actually breaks my heart into pieces that you were so alone through all of this. This is the part of our history I wish I could change. I wish I had been there for you. I wish I could have talked to you right after he abused you. I would have explained how wrong it was for him to do that.*

*I wish I could have been there when you were sexually acting out so I could gently explain that what you were doing was inappropriate and was a sign that something had happened to you and that we would get you help. But I can't. We can't go back there, baby girl.*

*The fact that you kept this pain and worry all to yourself for all those years and pretended to be okay is what hurts most. To me, **this** is the tragedy in the story of your life. But I am here now and I will never, ever leave you. Ever. I will listen to all of your fears and worries and instead of repressing you, I will encourage you to talk about them and I will try my best explain to you why you have them and comfort you.*

*But maybe you and I can use what has happened and help other kids, other children, other adults who have gone through similar things.*

*Maybe we can show them that no matter what happened, they are not irrevocably broken or bad. It was their abusers who were bad.*

*Maybe we can show them how to heal their souls even a little bit. Maybe we can turn all the darkness into light.*

*And guess what?*

*YOU, yes you, baby girl, are that light.*

The black dot I felt was on my soul was a constant reminder of how worthless and hopeless I was, how I would never find happiness. No matter what I did to try to scrub it out of my soul, it remained.

During one enlightening session, Dr. A. drew two pictures. One had a soul with a black dot inside it (representative of the past) and the other had a soul with a black dot outside of it (representing the present). Using this visual, he explained that the black dot I'd felt my entire life was THEIR sadness, THEIR shame, THEIR guilt, and THEIR craziness and I'd unfortunately absorbed all that as a child. All children, abused or not, internalize the emotions and behaviours of the adults around. It wasn't until he drew this visual that I realized I had been carrying around *their black dot, their issues,* inside *my* soul since childhood and had for all that time truly believed them to be mine. It was mind blowing. I saw everything so clearly.

I still ache over this. I mourn that a little girl absorbed other people's issues and made them her own. I am saddened that she viewed all this through an ignorant and uninformed adolescent perspective and then condemned herself without even knowing the truth. I grieve that she endured not only primary, but also secondary trauma because of them. Until recently, I thought I was to blame for my secondary trauma and my OCD-like thinking. I believed it was me that caused my secondary trauma, that it was my fault because of *my reaction* to the memories. Wrong. Even that wasn't my fault. I would have never experienced this horrific secondary trauma if it hadn't been for them or the religious beliefs I had been taught about an angry and vengeful god. So now I remind that little girl, when she feels sad that she caused such psychological devastation to herself because of her trauma, to let go of that lie and that sense of responsibility.

## LETTING GO

I wish I'd had the courage to speak out sooner than at the age of forty-three. Perhaps I wouldn't have become an alcoholic. Maybe if I'd had a voice it would have eliminated all those decades during which I walked around as a broken adult with unprocessed childhood emotions. Maybe I would have been a better mother, a better wife. But I am accepting that, for whatever reason, this was *my* journey in life. Now I choose to think that I had to go through all this so I could help someone else on his or her journey. I like to think that my pain will be turned into a huge gift and that one day I will meet someone exactly like me and I will be able alleviate her suffering by showing her how I found healing. I like to think that this painful process of writing my story will help others. We are human beings, which means we will experience suffering. It is what we do with the suffering that makes a difference. We can let it consume and devour us, darkening our light, as I once did, or we can accept it, search for the gifts within it, and become companions and guides to others who have experienced similar pain. If one chooses the latter, her suffering will become her greatest gift, just as mine has.

I have finally accepted that C-PTSD doesn't magically go away. Trust me, I have fought that battle long enough to know. I have wished it away, I have wrapped myself up in a blanket of self-pity, hating my life because I have this disorder. I have tried everything humanly possible to be rid of it. But how can I hate myself or my life for something that I didn't cause, that I didn't initiate? How can I hate myself because I am re-feeling the terror I once felt as a child and adolescent? No. I won't do that. I accept that my brain developed the way it did — with its arsenal of coping mechanisms — because of them. Not because of her or anything she did. I won't lie and say everything is perfect now. It isn't. There are days when I am overwhelmed about something and sometimes I feel as if I am right back there, nineteen years old, and sitting on those wooden steps having a complete nervous breakdown. And sadly, people with C-PTSD often have to fight two battles. One is what is actually happening at the moment. The other is the insidious reappearance of symptoms from the past trauma.

It is so easy for my brain to become overwhelmed when I am stressed. And when I become overwhelmed, I sometimes become symptomatic. Without my permission, without any invitation whatsoever, my trauma memories begin knocking on my mind's door again. Although I am no longer panicky, I am sad. I am angry. How dare these memories show up now when I am already anxious about something completely different? How dare they show up and overwhelm me when I need to be whole and healthy.

It is almost as if my C-PTSD holds out its hand and beckons me to rejoin it in that strange dance of despair. And as it patiently waits for me, I often have those emotional fear-based flashbacks and my old trauma thoughts taunt me: You are not strong enough. You are going to feel like this forever; the trauma will never end. You are bad. You're completely useless and a burden to your family. You are crazy, your brain isn't normal. And, finally, it whispers the death knell: Forget about your present stress, I am more important. Dance with me.

Fuck off.

Dr. A. taught me that when stress occurs, those of us with C-PTSD have to *constantly* reinforce the boundaries between the past and the present because our brains have problems differentiating between the two. I have to remind myself (and my inner child) that we are not back there, that we are dealing with a situation in the present and that the way we are reacting is normal for us. I will always have symptoms that can be triggered. That will never change. But, for the most part, I am okay with that because *today* I can choose how I will respond. Before recovery, I couldn't.

I do not need to accept my C-PTSD's invitation to dance. I can choose another partner. I can choose to dance with my inner child. Then we will sit down together and I will tell her how very sorry I am that she is still re-experiencing all those old emotions. I will tell her that I know she is strong enough to hear a truth. A truth that isn't fair yet needs to be accepted.

We might always become symptomatic when life gets overwhelming because of what happened. We might always *re-feel* the torturous thoughts, the memories, the feelings, and the lies she once believed. But she mustn't blame herself. Instead, she must allow herself to grieve that this happened. She must allow all those old fears, trauma thoughts, and feelings to pass *through us*. We can no longer run away from them. And as painful as the process of acceptance is, another layer will have been released.

I try to view this as the universe sending me a gift. It is the universe's way of saying that there is still an unmet need that my inner child has, some still-repressed energy she is still holding onto that needs to be released. It is a sign that she can heal a bit more. And I get to help her do that. I get another opportunity to become even closer to her.

This releasing is a process. It takes a long time. When she is ready, she opens her little hands and lets go of whatever it is, just a little bit. And the next time, she lets go of a little bit more. I don't push her or force her anymore, the way I used to. This now happens on her timing. Ironically, because I am now letting her heal at her own pace, it is happening faster. She used to be terribly afraid of her thoughts and memories, but now I have given her a free pass to think and remember anything. *Anything.* This is a very hard thing for me to do, but I believe that she has earned that right. And there is nothing she can remember that will ever break us apart.

In the beginning of my journey, this was a terrifying feat because when she initially didn't release everything all at once, I panicked. I went back to the old familiar emotion of helplessness and that my life would be like this forever. I was sure the war would soon resume in full force. So I remained stuck in that state of hypervigilance and didn't allow myself to feel joy or enjoy the present moment because I was so sure it wouldn't last.

But as time has passed, these ideas have softened. I now understand that my inner child is not going to automatically release decades-long repressions, fears, and old coping mechanisms all at once. For decades she BELIEVED to her very core that it was necessary to know everything in order to feel safe. This incessant need to know helped her predict and prevent whatever disaster she thought could befall her. Disasters she thought she was responsible for creating.

There are questions in life that can't never be answered and some that shouldn't be answered. But to a traumatized adolescent, this is unacceptable. She needs certainty. She craves it. Uncertainty spells disaster to her. And this need for certainty has carried into my adulthood.

Today, this remains one of my most severe symptoms. If I am unable to answer something, my mind automatically connects to that neural pathway my brain created in adolescence and screams, *"DANGER! You need to figure this out! You don't know! You are still not safe. Not knowing could mean disaster!!!!"*

This symptom has robbed me of that sense of wonder and awe of this beautiful planet, of this life. It has made me not want to think too deeply about anything.

This is very common in C-PTSD survivors. We fear our minds. We don't trust our minds. We certainly don't want to remember all the traumatic events and feelings and so we spend an extraordinary amount time avoiding anything to do with the memories. But as time goes by, this symptom, is starting to dissipate. I remind that girl that as a precious child of the universe, she has nothing to fear from her mind...what it contains are only *memories* of a war that was fought and that she won long ago.

I am learning that instead of going into panic mode and therefore allowing those neurons in my brain to start gearing up for battle, I remind her of the truth:

*Oh my precious girl. You are so lovely and you are SO smart. You always have been. I am so sorry that you fear your beautiful mind. But there is nothing to fear. It is perfectly normal and sane. The fears you have, the questions you NOW have are so futile, so irrelevant. They were needed back then when you were unsafe, but not anymore.*

*You are so safe.*

*You shouldn't be worrying that you can only be happy when you know everything is perfect, that everything is fixed.*

*No. I want you to look at me. You do NOT need to know everything is perfect in order to be happy. Nothing in this messy life is perfect. And that it isn't, and can't be, has nothing to do with you. THEY, put this idea in you... THEY put this "need to know" in you. It's just another thing that doesn't belong to you — so give it back.*

*Come on. Get up and let's go outside. Look around. Take it in. Think. Ponder. Wonder. Use your beautiful, perfectly normal and sane brain to come up with your OWN answers to things. No one can ever tell you what is right or what is wrong. You can trust your ideas. Whatever you come up with is perfect and beautiful and RIGHT because it comes from you and your truth.*

*Breathe in the majesty of this planet, the stars, and the trees and the birds soaring above your head. Look at all the incredible colours. Look at all the people. The colours, the diversity.*

*Don't be afraid. Give that fear back to them. It isn't your fear. It is not, nor ever was, part of your essence.*

*Be fearless and trust your ability to safely contemplate anything at all because I will always be walking right beside you. You can always ask me anything.*

*I will always remind you that sometimes the best part of life is in the NOT knowing, because then you can come up with whatever magical and beautiful conclusion YOU want. And your idea, and those conclusions you come up with, will always be correct because they are not based on your trauma and its misperceptions.*

*They are now based on the truth — your truth.*

I am beyond grateful for these conversations I continue to have and probably always will have with that beautiful warrior. They have turned out to be the solution to all my brokenness and confusion. Paradoxically, the answers were right inside me this entire time.

# CHAPTER
# *TWELVE*

## FORGIVENESS

As my mind has cleared and I have begun to heal from my past, I have accepted my diagnosis of C-PTSD at a core level. This is the hardest thing I have ever had to do in my life. It is far harder than accepting that I was an alcoholic. It is far harder than any abuse. It is the massive fallout, the life-long consequences I will always carry within me because of other people's actions. It just isn't fair. I am sobbing as I write this.

And I am realizing that even today, if I am open to it, my symptoms can offer huge insights — the learning never ends. In fact, recently I had a major one.

Two weeks ago, I went on beautiful trip with my husband to celebrate our anniversary. Although I was happy to be with him, I was also apprehensive because I don't like being too far from home. While we were away, there were many times I became completely overwhelmed with anxiety at the crowds of people and some of my old symptoms began to rear their ugly heads. I started feeling very unhappy that this was occurring in what should have been a lovely vacation. That old familiar yet powerful thought of "See, you may as well not even bother enjoying life because your trauma will always be there lurking, ready to strike" appeared.

I didn't completely panic though.

Instead, I intuitively knew that I needed to spend some time alone and sit with my spirit, my inner child. It was obvious she needed something from me.

As I connected with her, it became apparent that *she was sad.* She was asking *me* for forgiveness. I couldn't even imagine why she would be seeking this. I sensed she was seeking forgiveness for all the suffering that the maladaptive coping mechanisms were still causing me in the present. She was feeling once again that it was all her fault.

This epiphany broke my heart and I started sobbing. I was stunned. Imagine! After the way I shut her away for decades, she was asking *me* to forgive *her.*

>*Oh my beautiful baby girl. Of course I forgive you.*
>
>*I can't even believe that you are asking for my forgiveness, you don't need to even ask me for that. There is nothing to forgive, my love.*
>
>*I now fully understand why you acted the way you did, I understand why you ended up with all that fear and all those crazy coping mechanisms. And I don't blame you one bit.*
>
>*You did what you had to do to survive, honey.*
>
>*I am not mad at you. I need to know that I don't hold you responsible for ANY of this.*
>
>*I am going to be okay, baby girl. Momma is going to be okay. Don't you dare worry about me!*
>
>*Even if the symptoms or the intrusive thoughts or memories never go away, I am still going to be okay. Do I wish, for both our sakes, that everything could be erased, every memory, every thought, every moment of suffering? Of course I do, I won't lie to you. But,*

*honey, that is never going to happen and I am okay with that. And do you know why I am okay with it? Because I have you and you are the most precious thing about me. You have been one of my greatest teachers in this life.*

*You have taught me about human resilience, survival, and courage.*

*You are the one who taught me about self-love and who God really is. YOU did that. You used your pain to help me find that God that I had been seeking my entire life*

*Thank you for being courageous enough to tell me you needed me to forgive you. But there is absolutely no forgiveness needed, my love.*

*Just acceptance.*

# CHAPTER
# *THIRTEEN*

## THE GIFTS

I would not wish C-PTSD and/or addiction on anyone, including my abusers. I have known too many people who have lost their lives to both addiction and this soul-crushing brokenness.

Statistically, I am one of the lucky ones. But I've fought like hell to get to this place. I have realized as I continue to heal that this disorder has given me so many gifts — gifts that I think "normal" people may **never** receive while living on this planet.

First, it has afforded me the opportunity to smash my old idea of that punishing God.

No.

Never again will I believe in such a condemning, wrathful, and judging God. I have further promised myself that my own children will never grow up thinking that this is who their Creator is.

Letting go of this concept of God has been difficult, frightening and painful, though. I had to crush and unlearn that old God, that God of my *parents'* understanding, and choose my own Higher Power.

I had no idea where to even begin, so I kept it simple. I started asking the Universe, God, Creator, the Divine, whatever you want to call it, to reveal itself to me in the way that *I was supposed to know it. The way* I *needed to know it.* I did this every single morning. It has slowly over time, revealed itself as kindness, compassion, benevolence, comfort, and mainly, unconditional love. To me, it is like pure white energy smoldering in my heart. I cannot explain it, but I know and feel it exists. I no longer have any desire to know anyone else's concept of God. It doesn't matter to me. I now believe and trust in *our* truth. This will always be my answer to profound questions. I need a loving creator who will understand *me*, and my own personal issues right down to the very core of my being, my soul…where she lives. As I continued to experience this presence, this comforting and loving energy, I ask that it continue to heal the shattered and splintered pieces of that little girl because there are still times when she is hurting. Some days I don't have a clue about how to even pick up her pieces without cutting myself. And guess what's happened? This benevolent divinity has taken my hand, and taken her hand, and joined us together. And It whispered, *you have the power to heal each other.*

Today I do not believe that God caused my abuse or my own self-inflicted suffering. Human beings did. Imperfect, fallible human beings. My Twelve Step sponsor, who is also a survivor of childhood sexual abuse, always reminds me: If I put the Divine's Light and Love in the middle of this or any messy tragedy life throws my way, I can ask that the pain be used for a higher purpose. If I do this, miracles can and will come out of it. I am proof of that. Today, I journey with many women who have had very similar experiences and it's absolutely humbling and fulfilling.

How blessed am I that after all I have been through, I have gone from thinking my creator absolutely despised me and was going to punish me for eternity to uncovering such a loving Divinity whom I know will shelter me from ANY storm? I know I will never be alone again.

I believe that it is THIS God who is now with me and my inner child when my C-PTSD flashbacks take me back to that dark wooden childhood closet, to my cousin's bedroom with its flowered wallpaper, to my dad's old green chair. It sits with me on those wooden stairs on that rainy October night and comforts me. I don't need to go to any church to find this Divine Being. It lives inside my heart. Right next to her.

The second gift C-PTSD has given me is the most profound connection to my inner child. It amazes me that there was a time in my life when I wanted NOTHING to do with her and I despised her. Now, her courage and resilience absolutely amaze me. She lived through physical abuse, sexual abuse, abandonment, and then unspeakable secondary trauma. Yet she kept going. She kept fighting. She kept knocking on the door of my soul for decades until I opened it. And when I finally opened it, she was so battered and bruised and exhausted from the war she had fought, that it took a lot of time to trust, believe, and fall in love with each other. But we did it. Together.

As mentioned, I am now acutely aware that when I am triggered, it is because she, my little girl, needs something. I am learning not to react traumatically, as I did in the past, but instead to take the time to quiet my mind, to go to her and find out what is upsetting her.

Most of the time she just needs to be comforted. Sometimes, I symbolically hold her by holding the stuffed animal that The Gatehouse gave me when I started their program. I encourage her to feel and to let go. I allow her to bawl or rage and scream at the unfairness of it all. I take *her* lead. I do not repress anything.

Most times, she just needs to be reminded about how precious and beautiful she really is and that those intense traumatic feelings and memories are only C-PTSD symptoms, nothing more. The past is over, the war has been fought and she was victorious. She found me. She found her God. She found her truth. And in her I found my soul.

And when I really think about it, we are healing each other. She is the most amazing little warrior I know, and she's all mine.

A few years ago, my daughter and I went back to my childhood home. I hadn't been there in fifteen years. I was just starting my recovery journey and I wanted to see my old house again. I actually rang the doorbell to ask if I could just peek inside and show my daughter. A man answered the door, I explained who we were and why we were there. He emphatically said, "No, you absolutely cannot come in this house."

I asked if I could at least see the backyard where my dad took such care and pride, tending to his garden and roses. The man relented. I entered the backyard and was utterly shocked at what I saw. All my father's rose bushes were gone, the garden was dead, and there was actual trash all over the lawn. It broke my heart. There was not a trace of any of the effort my dad had put into his garden. I started to cry.

In that moment I knew it was over.

Symbolically, my daughter could have been my inner child and the Universe did not want that inner child in that house anymore. She was not allowed to go back in the house where she would see the rooms where she was sometimes hit and see the closet where she used to hide. She did not need to see the living room where that old green chair was. The chair where her father hid behind his newspaper and drank, the chair where she read that Bible verse and was completely abandoned by me and by that old version of God. She was not supposed to walk down those wooden stairs where she once sat and believed that her life was completely over.

And the childhood memories of that perfect green lawn, the gorgeous perennial garden, and all the massive rose bushes we had, were now transformed into what I now know is the truth of my past: one big fucking mess and total destruction.

Thank God the man told us to leave.

Complex-PTSD has also given me a sense of compassion and empathy that most people do not possess. Sadly, our world has become so self-centered that we have forgotten why we are here. It is not about what we look like or about acquiring and having possessions. It is about authentic human and spiritual connection. It is about using our gifts, which sometimes appear in the form of tragedy, to help others. It is about building people up instead of tearing them down. Finally, it is about peeling back the layers of our painful human experiences and finding our way back to the truth and, therefore, to the Divine within ourselves.

I now have profound compassion for those who suffer any type of abuse and want to use my experience to offer hope and help light their way to find their own inner truth. Although I can't tell anyone which road they are supposed to travel to get there, I can offer them hope that the human spirit can never, ever be broken. It lives on forever and its spark can never be extinguished, no matter what one endures. As one survivor recently taught me, when our light is dimmed, others can help shine their light into us and help us restore our brightness to where it was always meant to be.

We all need each other. We need connection, not isolation. When we are connected, we find that all our broken pieces fit perfectly into one another and we become a beautiful mosaic.

I can offer insight and become a companion on this journey if a person needs one.

It is the least I can do after all the universe has given me.

Finally, Complex-PTSD provided me with a whole tribe of people to help me in this lifetime: this tribe includes my husband, my children, Anne, Dr. A., my dog (who is really just a soul with fur) and a very small, select group of the most beautiful friends.

I have gone from living in complete isolation to slowly allowing these people to see me for who I really am. This tribe surrounds me, protects me, and loves me despite all my brokenness, imperfections, cracks, and mistakes. They all know my entire story and not one of them has judged me or walked away as I once feared they would.

Who gets such a gift?

Most people, I know, will never come close to having the kind of profound, soul-level relationships with others who have experienced similar struggles that I am now blessed to have.

And it is all thanks to C-PTSD and its ensuing addiction.

Imagine.

Actually, part of the reason I began writing this was for my husband and children, because no matter how hard I tried or wanted to, they never got a fully present mother or wife, especially during the early days. I was too busy in my head — I was still obsessing, scanning, and searching for signs of potential danger that no longer existed. I was terrified that I was going to become like my abusers. I felt so unworthy of my husband and children that I often withdrew from certain activities to try to protect them. And when the craziness in my head became too much, I drank.

I was completely absent for two years of their lives. And this will ALWAYS be my biggest regret.

I hope when I am gone from this life, this writing may give them an understanding as to why I was the way I was. I desperately need them to know it was THEM, all three of them, who have helped me heal in ways that cannot adequately be explained. Just their presence, their quiet understanding, their hugs and encouragement, have helped me climb the enormous mountain of my recovery. They have been the wind beneath my broken wings.

Ironically, when I first started this journey, my family took a trip to Blue Mountain in Collingwood. It was the day Robin Williams committed suicide and I was overcome with empathy and sorrow for him. While the world was in shock over his death, I understood completely why he ended his beautiful life.

My young children begged me to climb to the top of the mountain with them. It was the last thing I wanted to do. I agreed even though I was wearing flip-flops instead of running shoes.

This experience has now become a metaphor of sorts and thus, the title for this book.

The terrain was terrible, there were rocks and tall grass everywhere. I kept slipping and falling because of the ridiculous flip-flops I was wearing. I started crying out of sheer frustration and exhaustion, not because of the physical climb itself, but the metaphorical climb of my suffering.

In that moment, it seemed all my life I had been trying to climb Mount Everest in flip-flops.

But my beautiful children kept running on ahead me, yelling, "Mommy, Mommy! You can do it!! Keep going! Follow us." With tears streaming down my face, I neared the top of the mountain and told them I didn't think I would make it. I kept slipping. They stuck their little hands out and pulled me to the top and told me emphatically that I had made it!

They yelled, "We knew you could do it, Mommy!"

And I did.

And I have.

And the view from the top is pretty spectacular.

# CHAPTER
# FOURTEEN

## JOY

I once read that a human being's natural state is joy. Not fear, worry, or sadness, but joy. I also read that infants begin to show the first signs of happiness by the time they are three months old.

I don't even know what that word means, what it feels like, or what it is. But I have always been driven to search for it. The other day, while I was speaking with other survivors, someone said, "I feel like I have had to work at finding joy my entire life." Everyone, including me, nodded in agreement. Joy is not *our* natural state and, therefore, when it *is* felt, it can be foreign and terrifying. In fact, some of us would prefer to just stay in our familiar state of existing in pain rather than risk embracing this feeling.

But what is joy?

After my traumatic breakdown and complete self-abandonment, I began to look for things outside myself that I assumed would bring me joy, this happiness, this sense of contentment.

I landed my dream job as a teacher. I loved that job. I loved the children and their curiosity, and I especially loved their purity. I loved my colleagues, but still there was a disconnection, a lingering sense of unfulfillment, of sadness.

Later, I thought maybe if I got married, if I found someone to love me unconditionally, I would find this elusive joy. I began dating and found a man who was completely selfless, caring, and kind. I married *that* man, and not a man similar to my abusers, which is the norm for many of us. I do remember feeling almost blissful after our wedding ceremony. I was so happy. It was beautiful. But the feeling was fleeting.

The biggest shock I experienced in my search for joy was when I gave birth to my first child. I was positive children were going to be that missing puzzle piece in my life. I knew it was going to be *them*, my own biological children that I would grow and carry inside me, that would bring me a deep sense of fulfillment, purpose, and joy. I became pregnant as soon as we began trying. I absolutely could not wait for the birth, for that very moment when the doctor would hand me my child. In my ignorance, this was going to be the exact second when everything within me would be fixed.

I went into labour and delivered my firstborn. He was placed on my chest and I felt … nothing. It was as if I was completely detached. There was no joy, but there was no unhappiness either. There was no anything. It was as if I didn't know what to do, what to feel. I tried searching for this feeling of joy while he lay in my arms but it wasn't there. I smiled at all my loved ones surrounding me, but I was terrified at my lack of emotion. I dared not tell anyone because I was afraid of being judged, afraid that I was heartless. Afraid I wouldn't be able to nurture this beautiful child. I was so numb. My brain could not fathom how I could create a life and give birth to a beautiful baby — *my own baby* — and yet feel nothing. What I didn't realize was that my past experiences, my traumas, had robbed me of that primary emotion. I was literally *incapable* of feeling joy even during the most beautiful and profound experiences in life. This is yet another thing I have had to grieve.

When I have shared this experience in various groups, I have learned just how common it is. Many women say they also experienced this disconnection when they gave birth. Tragically, some trauma survivors have told me they have chosen not to become parents because they feel they don't deserve to have children. Others are terrified of bringing a child into a world that only knows abuse, loss, and tragedy. And still others think they are completely incapable of raising a child. Can you imagine? We are already robbed of so many things in this life because of our abuse. To then be denied the opportunity to become a parent is unimaginable to me. It is a crime. And trust me, the women and men I have met on my journey are people who are compassionate, empathetic, and loving to a fault. They would make such beautiful parents if given the chance to heal from their own wounds.

In my own case, my love for my children did grow after that initial feeling of detachment. And today, that love is all-consuming. I would do anything for my children. Have I made mistakes? Yes. Have I done the best I could? I used to think I hadn't but today, when I look at my entire life story, I know I have. My children have witnessed their mother face every challenge imaginable head-on. Yes, they have witnessed my pain, but they have also witnessed my determination to heal. My children have learned the value of never giving up.

Having my children didn't fill that void, that emptiness and sadness. They could not give me the joy that I could only find in myself. And so, my search for this emotion continued.

Now that I have healed and found love with my inner child, the strangest thing has happened. I believe I am beginning to feel joy at the smallest things. Sunrises. Stars. Animals. Children. Rainbows. Friendships. Nature. I am finding things that I truly like to do and that I am actually good at. For the first time in my *entire life* I am feeling passion and excitement about doing them. Still, there are moments I feel guilty and afraid of this feeling. I feel weird. I get scared. Am I *allowed* to feel this feeling of joy? What if it doesn't last? What if it is taken away? What if I have a flashback that lasts for weeks and overrides this new feeling? Part of my brain tells me maybe it's better just to remain in my natural state of nothingness. Then I can't lose anything. I am learning to stop and go to *her* and remind her that she is finally free to soar. I tell her that she is allowed to feel this feeling and be creative and recapture all the joy that she was robbed of decades ago. I remind her that joy is her *natural* state. She is not supposed to be afraid.

> *Oh my sweet baby girl.*
> *I know you struggle with finding joy, with finding happiness.*
> *I think you have become so numb, so detached that you don't even know what those words mean, let alone if they are attainable.*
> *Honey, every single child is born with joy, but you were robbed of it. Robbed. Your abusers stole that emotion right out of your precious soul.*
> *You internalized and absorbed so many negative and shame-based messages from them that happiness became an illusion, something completely unreachable.*
> *You have known only very fleeting moments of happiness because most of your energy has been spent in worry and fear.*
> *This is not how a child is supposed to feel.*
> *I need you to listen to me.*
> *I know there was a time when you truly thought you didn't deserve to be happy. You thought you were so immoral, so broken and beyond repair.*
> *But you know the truth now.*
> *You are and were always pure, innocent, beautiful, and deserving of so much joy.*
> *Let me bring joy into your soul every single day.*

*Ask the Divine, the universe, to guide you because more than anyone else, you deserve to feel happiness.*

*You have suffered enough.*

*I want you to welcome the benevolence of this universe to help you rediscover that birthright.*

*Ask it to illuminate the way for you and help purge your spirit of all those old worries and fears and replace them with joy.*

*You can do it.*

*Mama will be with you every step of the way. I am not going anywhere.*

*There is no one else I'd rather discover this with than you, my love.*

My new hobby is sourcing out old furniture, refinishing and repainting it with personal designs, stencils, and awesome details. It brings me so much joy. I sometimes wake up in the middle of the night thinking about a piece that I'm working on and how I can make it more interesting and lovely. I used to wake up and think only of my trauma.

Gratitude is not a big enough word. I am so grateful to this universe and its Creator who took a discarded piece of furniture (me) and saw something beautiful in it, despite its appearance. I am grateful my Creator tirelessly worked on it and refined and remolded it into something magnificent. Something full of unique details and intricacies.

I used to think this universe was unkind and cold and meaningless. Now I know it has *always* been on my side and has been ceaselessly removing any object that was preventing me from feeling my birthright — joy.

It is effortless now. It just kind of comes. I am slowly letting go of my fear of it. And every day I am thankful for it.

Joy. Wow.

For comments or further information, Diana Sumner
can be reached at dianasumner33@gmail.com

Printed in the United States
By Bookmasters